Schwalm Embroidery

TECHNIQUES AND DESIGNS

Christine Bishop

MILNER CRAFT SERIES

First published in 1999 by
Sally Milner Publishing Pty Ltd
PO Box 2104
Bowral NSW 2576

Reprinted 2000

Design Anna Warren, Warren Ventures, Sydney
Illustration by Christine Bishop
Photography by Christine Bishop
Printed and bound in China

National Library of Australia
Cataloguing-in-Publication data:

    Bishop, Christine.
    Schwalm embroidery techniques and designs.

    ISBN 1 86351 220 9

    1. Embroidery - Germany - Schwalm River Region (Hesse) -
    Methodology. 2. Embroidery - Germany - Schwalm River
    Region (Hesse) - Patterns. 1. Title. (Series : Milner craft series).

    746.44

CONTENTS

INTRODUCTION

Schwalm is named after the region along the Schwalm River, known as 'die Schwalm'. The town most associated with this embroidery is Schwalmstadt, formerly known as Ziegenhain, which lies approximately 30kms (20 miles) north east of Marburg, Germany.

Schwalm is a form of late eighteenth to nineteenth century whitework embroidery which incorporates surface stitches, pulled fabric, drawn thread, needlelace and needleweaving, and was traditionally embroidered on blouses, shirts and stockings, pillowcases, top sheets and towels. Traditional design elements are based on the 'tree of life'. These include hearts, tulips, the sun, pine cones, flowers, fruit, leaves, tendrils and the pigeon or dove.

Before World War 2, it was considered essential for girls to be taught embroidery and at a very young age they would be either apprenticed to a master embroiderer or taught by older members of their family. They were expected to begin their married life with all the necessary embroidered household linen as part of their dowry.

The original Schwalm embroidery closely resembles the earliest form of Hedebo from Denmark, in that the treatment of the design elements and the stitches are similar. (*See Plates 1 and 2*) Old Hedebo design elements are surrounded by two rows of chain stitch, whereas in Schwalm embroidery, they are usually first surrounded by a row of chain, then a row of coral stitch outside the chain stitch. Additional rows of embroidery can be added in Schwalm embroidery. These could include a row of herringbone or chevron stitch, followed by another row of coral stitch and finally a row of buttonhole semicircles, pyramids or straight stitches grouped in various combinations. In the earlier examples of both Hedebo and Schwalm, the fabric would be completely covered with embroidery to prevent the release of evil spirits through the fabric — this is sometimes referred to as abhorrence of the void.

Similarities can also be found with eighteenth century Dresden embroidery, although with Dresden embroidery the flowing floral designs were worked upon a fine cotton muslin and only filled with pulled fabric embroidery. (*See Plate 3*)

Thekla Gombert and Käthe Hartenbach, master embroiderers from Schwalmstadt-Ziegenhain, were responsible for the revival of Schwalm embroidery. Thekla and Käthe produced many beautiful traditional whitework designs which were published in early editions of the *Anna Burda* magazine. Sadly, Thekla died a few years ago but she has left a wonderful legacy of embroidery which will remain an inspiration for many.

Schwalm was usually worked with white threads on white linen, however, for the photography for this book only, coloured linen and ecru threads have been used for all projects. Feel free to use either the traditional white or coloured linens.

DESIGN ELEMENTS AND
THEIR MEANING

The tree of life is found in many forms of art and can be interpreted as a symbol of immortality or as a symbol of heaven at the end of the world. Embroideries from both Germany and Italy depict the tree cross which is an interpretation of the Cross of Christ. This tree usually has leaves, blossoms and fruits as a symbol of the overcoming of death.

The heart is generally regarded as a symbol of love and friendship. The tulip can be representative of the relationship between the sun, rain and life itself. In German speaking lands the sun is warming, nourishing and maternal. Pine cones are a fertility symbol and are closely related to the tree of life.

In ancient Germany a dark dove was regarded as a bird of the spirit and sometimes the spirit of death and misfortune. However, I would prefer the alternative description of the dove as being a sign of peace and hope.

BASIC TECHNIQUES AND REQUIREMENTS

TRANSFERRING THE DESIGN

To transfer the design onto the fabric, lightly trace onto tissue, tracing or kitchen paper, the entire design or section of the design as indicated in the instructions for individual projects. Next, using a medium tone tacking thread and running stitch, stitch through the paper and the fabric. When the design is completely transferred to the fabric, run a sharp needle along the running stitch to perforate the paper. Carefully tear away the paper from the fabric.

Note: Begin the running stitch with a knot and make sure the ends are secure in the fabric, otherwise your stitching will be removed when you tear the paper away from the fabric.

Note on tacking thread

Do not be tempted to use a very dark tacking thread such as black, navy or red. Moisture in the air may cause dyes in the thread to run and leave marks on your fabric, while a thread the same colour as your fabric may be difficult to see. This is why I recommend a medium tone thread.

HOW TO BEGIN AND END THREADS

Refer to diagram in stitch Glossary.

A waste knot is a knot at the end of your thread that will be later cut away so that you can finish off the thread neatly on the back of your work. Knot the end of your thread and pass the needle down through the fabric (so that the knot is on the front of the fabric) approximately 8cm (3¼") from where you wish to begin your embroidery and where it will not become tangled on the back of your work.

When you have used the thread, cut away the waste knot and secure the end of the thread on the back of the work by weaving it through the back of 2 or 3 stitches, then 1 backstitch, splitting the thread to 'lock' the stitch. Cut away any excess thread.

NEEDLES
Use No 7 crewel needle for coral stitch (it is easier to pick up one thread of the fabric with a sharp needle) and use a No 22 tapestry needle for all other embroidery. Remember needle sizes and quality vary depending on the brand. The above sizes are based on Piecemaker needles.

ABBREVIATIONS/TERMS USED
WEFT = horizontal fabric threads,
WARP = vertical fabric threads,
Broder = Coton-à-Broder

HEIRLOOM CLOTH

Centre design measures 58cm (23″) x 58cm (23″). The design can be adapted easily to a rectangle or a larger square.

TECHNIQUES

Include surface stitches, pulled fabric, drawn thread work and needleweaving. A decorative border surrounds the centre design which features 13 different filling stitches. The cloth has a hemstitched hem and mitred corners.

REQUIREMENTS

140cm (56″) by 140cm (56″) of 30/32 count close weave linen or size required (photograph shows Permin antique pink 32 count linen)
2 skeins of No 12 ecru Coton-à-Broder
3 skeins of No 16 ecru Coton-à-Broder
3 skeins of No 20 ecru Coton-à-Broder
1 skein of No 25 ecru Coton-à-Broder
No 24 tapestry needle
No 7 crewel needle
Medium tone tacking thread
Tracing paper or similar and pencil
15cm (6″) round embroidery frame

DESIGN
The centre embroidery measures 51.5cm (43″) square. The design can be adapted to a rectangle by

the addition of a flower on 2 sides only, or the square can be reduced by the removal of one flower from each side.

PREPARING YOUR FABRIC
Overlock, oversew or zigzag around the edge to prevent the linen from fraying. Fold the fabric in half horizontally and mark this fold line with a tacking thread. Fold the fabric in half vertically and mark this fold line with a tacking thread. The dotted line on the design sheets measures 58cm (23") square — mark with a pin on all 4 tacking lines, 29cm (11½") out from the centre of the fabric. Outline the 58cm (23") square with a tacking thread. To ensure your tacking lines are accurate measure across from one corner of the square to the opposite corner — it should read 68cm (27").

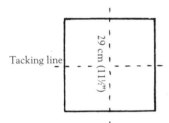

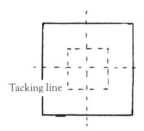

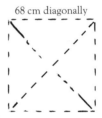

STITCHES
Refer pages which follow, and Stitch Glossary.
   Surface stitches include chain, coral, straight (single satin stitch), herringbone and interlacing (or threaded) over herringbone stitch and buttonhole stitch. Pulled fabric and drawn thread stitches and fillings include four sided stitch, overcast eyelets, antique hemstitch, step stitch filling, cross stitch, single feather stitch, needleweaving on lattice stitch, honeycomb stitch, rose stitch (drawn filling — Russian), and dove's eye stitch (some books refer to this as Greek cross filling stitch).

TRANSFERRING YOUR DESIGN
Copy the design sheet 4 times and place the sheets to form a square as in diagram on page 13. Secure the sheets and lightly trace the design outline and outer dotted line onto tissue paper. Pin the tissue

DESIGN SHEET HEIRLOOM CLOTH
Copy 4 times

Enlarge at 134% on a photocopier

Fold along this
line only

paper onto the fabric and align the outer dotted lines with the tacking thread on the fabric. These must be accurate before you commence transferring the design. When you are sure all lines align, using a tacking thread and running stitch, stitch through the tissue paper and the fabric. When you have completed the running stitch, run a sharp needle along the running stitch which will perforate the paper. Carefully tear the paper away from the fabric. You are now ready to begin.

Note: If you wish to alter the centre embroidery to a rectangle, either remove flowers 1 and 5 for a small rectangle or repeat No 4 and add a French

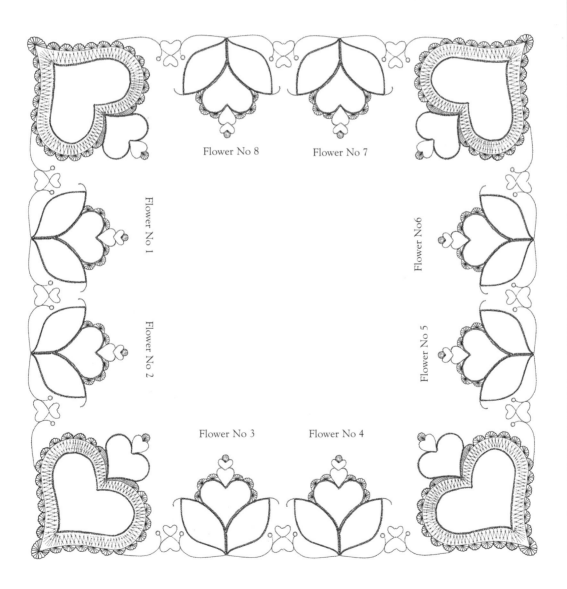

Flower No 8 Flower No 7

Flower No 1

Flower No 2

Flower No6

Flower No 5

Flower No 3 Flower No 4

knot in each of the diamonds formed by the honeycomb stitch, and repeat No 1 by adding a cross
stitch in the void between the diagonal satin stitch
fillings for a larger rectangle.

METHOD OF WORKING THE DESIGN

Work the design in the following order:

1. Corner hearts and flowers — all surface stitchery i.e. chain stitch, coral stitch, satin stitch, buttonhole stitch semi-circles, herringbone stitch
   and eyelets.
2. Flowers — fillings in the correct order from 1 to
   8 as there are 8 different fillings.
3. Corner hearts — fillings, all four are identical

SURFACE STITCHERY — ALL FLOWERS
Outline the flowers first with chain stitch using No
16 Broder and No 24 tapestry needle, then with
coral stitch using No 12 Broder and No 7 crewel
needle outside the chain stitch.

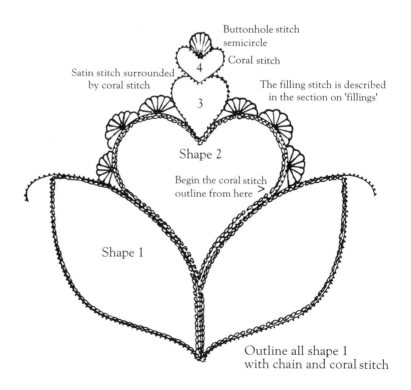

Buttonhole stitch
semicircle

Coral stitch

Satin stitch surrounded
by coral stitch

The filling stitch is described
in the section on 'fillings'

Shape 2

Begin the coral stitch
outline from here

Shape 1

Outline all shape 1
with chain and coral stitch

Note: Where the heart shape (No 2) extends into the centre of the flower, there is only one row of coral stitch.

Outline the 2 small hearts (Nos 3 & 4) with coral stitch using No 12 Broder. While you have No 12 Broder in the needle, embroider satin stitch in shape No 3.

Embroider buttonhole stitch semicircles along the top of shape No 2 using No 16 Broder. While you have No 16 Broder in the needle, embroider the buttonhole stitch fan on top of shape No 4, weaving the thread carefully on the back of the work from one area to the next.

'Top and tail' hearts, trailing and eyelet border linking the flowers with the corner hearts. Outline the hearts with coral stitch using No 12 Broder. The trailing is embroidered using No 12 Broder and coral stitch. The overcast eyelet is embroidered using No 20 Broder.

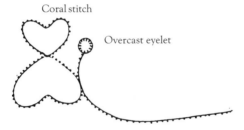

Coral stitch

Overcast eyelet

Eyelets

Eyelets are usually worked by outlining the shape with running stitch, however in Schwalm you can choose to either outline all the circle or begin with only a few running stitches as in the diagrams on the next page.

Using No 20 Broder, begin with 3 running stitches on or inside the tacking thread working from right to left, then begin the overcast stitch working back over the running stitches to secure the beginning of the thread. Remember, with over-cast stitch eyelets the needle should go down through the centre of the eyelet and up outside the tacking thread and running stitches. Ease the thread away from the centre of the eyelet to form the hole. The stitches should be next to one another in the centre not crossed over or twisted. If you find it

Outline all the eyelet

or begin with only a few running sts

difficult to achieve a neat eyelet try placing the stitches further apart and always pointing towards the centre of the circle.

To complete each eyelet, loosen off the last 3 stitches and run the needle under these stitches on the back of the work to secure the end of the thread. Tighten these 3 stitches and cut the thread. I was taught this method of finishing off by Mrs Enid Holds and I have found this to be the best method of completing eyelets without having to struggle to pull the needle through firm stitches and distorting the eyelet.

front of the eyelet

back of the eyelet

SURFACE STITCHERY — CORNER HEARTS

Before beginning the surface stitchery, you should have 2 rows of tacking stitch to outline the large heart shape. Inside the inner tacking thread, outline the large heart shape with chain stitch and No 16 Broder. Outside this chain stitch, embroider coral stitch with No 12 Broder. Outside the outer tacking thread embroider another row of coral stitch. Between the 2 rows of coral stitch embroider her-ringbone stitch with No 16 Broder.

Note: Begin at the top of the heart. Herringbone stitch is usually embroidered in a straight line, however, to embroider this stitch in a curve, allow a larger space between the stitches on the outer edge of the curve.

At the base of the heart embroider one stitch into the point. To achieve this, pick up 1 or 2 threads of the fabric for 3 stitches above the point and continue with the herringbone stitch along the other side of the heart, matching the density of stitches on both sides.

Buttonhole stitch
semicircles

Coral stitch

Chain stitch

Coral stitch

See 'fillings' for
stitch details

See 'fillings' for
stitch details

Chain stitch

Coral stitch

Herringbone stitch
threaded

Buttonhole stitch
semicircles

All corner hearts

To complete the herringbone stitch row a heavier thread (No 12 Broder) is threaded over the intersection of the threads as follows:

The interlacing thread does not pierce the fabric

Outline the smaller heart first with chain stitch and then with coral stitch and outline the smallest heart only with coral stitch. The buttonhole stitch semicircle is embroidered using No 16 Broder. Complete the last row of the large heart now with buttonhole stitch semicircles also using No 16 Broder, accentuating the point of the heart with a 3/4 circle. Begin this row at the top of the heart with approximately 12 straight buttonhole stitches then begin the first semicircle.

FILLING STITCHES — FLOWERS
All 8 flowers have four-sided stitches in shape No 2 using No 20 Broder over 3 fabric threads x 3 fabric threads. Compensate for half stitches on the curves. Begin the four-sided stitch in the centre where indicated.

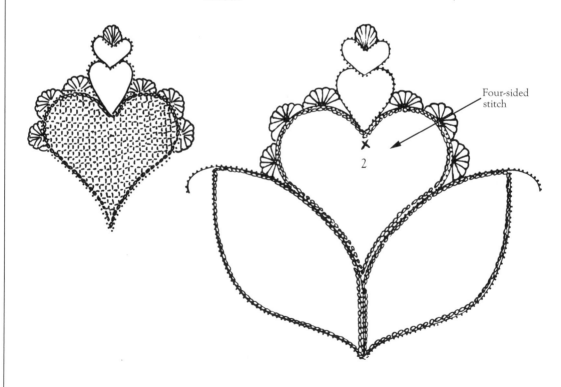

Four-sided stitch

After you have completed the four sided stitches filling on all 8 flowers, embroider the fillings working from Nos. 1–8. Some fillings have threads cut and withdrawn to form a grid.

How to form a grid

Leave the threads indicated on each diagram, cut the number of threads indicated and turn the fabric over to the wrong side. Withdraw the cut thread back to the edge with a blunt needle and cut it as close as possible to the edge. When you turn your work to the front you should have a neat edge with no 'whiskers' showing around the edge.

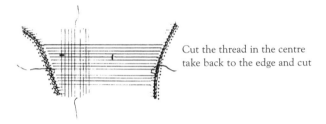

Cut the thread in the centre take back to the edge and cut

Fillings — Flower no 1

Withdraw 1 fabric thread and leave 6 fabric threads both warp (vertical) and weft (horizontal) as indicated on the diagram. The same thread should be withdrawn on both sides (mirror image).

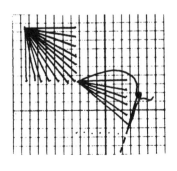

Note on removing threads: Be careful when removing threads as the centre where the sections meet is only held together with one row of coral stitch and two rows of chain. If you have difficulty with the fabric use a matching sewing thread to backstitch between the coral and chain stitches.

Embroider satin stitch fans beginning at the top left corner, diagonally to the centre of the flower, using No 20 Broder. Compensate for half stitches around the edge of the curves.

Fillings — Flower no 2

Withdraw 1 fabric thread and leave 4 fabric threads both warp and weft. Remove the same threads on both sides (mirror image).

Work from left to right

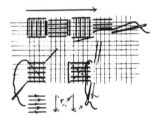

After working the 5 satin stitches over 4 fabric threads, complete the stitch by working the vertical arms of four-sided stitch. Commence the next block of 5 satin stitches.

Embroider step stitch surrounded by four-sided stitch using No 20 Broder. (Step stitch is used in pulled work but I have been unable to find a name for this variation.)

Fillings — Flower no 3

Withdraw 2 fabric threads and leave 2 fabric threads both warp and weft as indicated on the diagram, taking care when removing threads and, again, the sides should be a mirror image.

First embroider lattice stitch diagonally across the withdrawn thread grid, followed by the needlewoven filling using No 16 Broder. The needleweaving is worked from the top left corner towards the centre for the left petal and the opposite for the right petal.

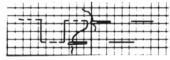

Work lattice stitch first then needleweave over the lattice stitch.

Fillings — Flower no 4

Withdraw 1 fabric thread and leave 3 fabric threads weft only (horizontal). The same threads should be withdrawn on both sides (mirror image).

Gently pull the thread so that a hole appears

Embroider honeycomb filling stitch beginning in the top left or right corner using No 16 Broder. Compensate for half stitches around the edge of the curves.

Fillings — Flower no 5

Withdraw 1 fabric thread and leave 6 fabric threads both warp and weft. Withdraw the same threads both sides to form a mirror image.

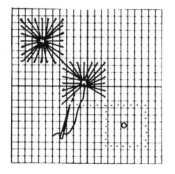

Embroider Algerian eye stitch over the square of 6 fabric threads x 6 fabric threads using No 25 Broder. The centre of the stitch is pulled slightly to form a hole similar to an eyelet. Compensate for half stitches around the edge of the curves.

Fillings — Flower no 6

Withdraw 1 fabric thread and leave 3 fabric threads both warp and weft. Remove the same threads on both sides (mirror image).

Using No 20 Broder and beginning at the top left corner, embroider lattice stitch diagonally towards the centre of the flower. Take the thread under the centre of the flower and work the same stitch up the other side to the opposite corner.

Also in No 20 Broder embroider dove's eye stitch in the next row and lattice stitch in the next. The alternating stitches forms the pattern.

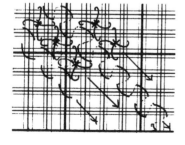

Fillings — Flower no 7

Withdraw 1 fabric thread and leave 4 fabric threads both warp and weft. The same threads should be withdrawn on both sides to form a mirror image.

Using No 20 Broder embroider step stitch over the block of 4 fabric threads x 4 fabric threads working diagonally from top left corner to the centre of the flower. Miss one block of 4 fabric threads and work diagonally across the next. Embroider a cross stitch over the 4 fabric thread block between the step stitches. Work the cross stitch vertically rather than diagonally, otherwise the carried thread is visible from the front.

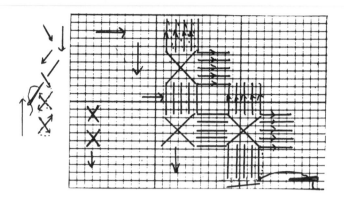

When embroidering the cross stitches work the stitches first one way then the other, slipping the needle under the thread every other stitch.

Fillings — Flower no 8

Withdraw 1 fabric thread and leave 3 fabric threads weft only (horizontal). Remove the same threads on both sides (mirror image).

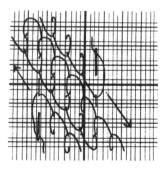

Using No 16 Broder embroider single feather stitch diagonally from the top left corner to the centre of the flower working over 3 fabric threads x 3 fabric threads for each stitch. The second or locking row of single feather stitch is worked by turning your embroidery upside down and embroidering back to where you started your first stitch.

1 Example of Old Hedebo

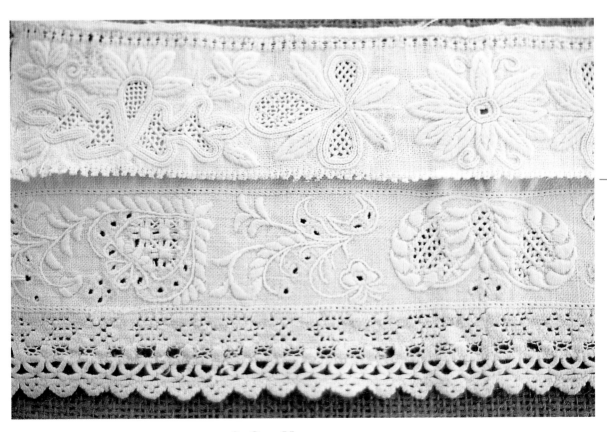

2 Old Hedebo cuffs

3 18TH CENTURY DRESDEN EMBROIDERY

4 HEIRLOOM CLOTH

5. DETAIL —
HEIRLOOM CLOTH
CORNER HEART

6. DETAIL —
HEIRLOOM CLOTH FLOWER 1

7. DETAIL —
HEIRLOOM CLOTH FLOWER 2

FILLINGS — CORNER HEARTS

Complete the *smaller* of the hearts first with step
stitch working 10 satin stitches over 3 fabric
threads. Begin where indicated at the top of the
heart and establish one complete row. Then 'fill in'
the two curved areas above the foundation row, followed by the remaining rows below. Compensate
for half stitches around the curved edges. Complete
this stitch in all four corners before proceeding on
to the large heart filling.

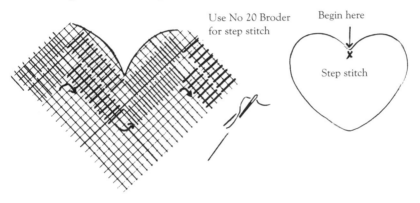

Use No 20 Broder
for step stitch

Begin here

Step stitch

Large Corner Hearts

To form the grid withdraw 2 fabric threads and
leave 2 fabric threads both warp and weft.

Embroider rose stitch (drawn filling — Russian) on the grid working from top left diagonally to the bottom right side of the heart. See Stitch Glossary.

EDGE BAND

At this stage you may have to adjust the tacking thread around the edge of the design. (You may not have the same number of threads from the edge of the design to the proposed border on every corner). Count the threads and run a new tacking thread. Use a tape measure or ruler to gauge the distance.

Work the inner row first. Cut and withdraw 4 fabric threads within the end tacking lines on all four sides, leaving sufficient thread to weave back into the hem (10cm, 4"). Take the thread back an additional 8 fabric threads and leave (these will be woven into the hem after you have withdrawn all the threads).

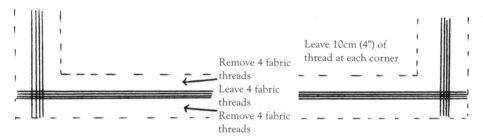

Leave 10cm (4") of thread at each corner

Remove 4 fabric threads

Leave 4 fabric threads

Remove 4 fabric threads

Leave 4 fabric threads outside the above and withdraw another 4 fabric threads. Weave the threads back into what will be covered by a buttonhole stitch corner.

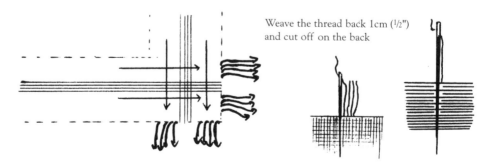

Weave the thread back 1cm (½") and cut off on the back

Embroider antique hemstitching on the inside first, over 3 fabric threads x 3 fabric threads using No 25 Broder. Count the threads close to the edge and adjust approximately 2cm (⁴/₅") from the corner if necessary.

Then embroider antique hemstitching on the outer edge of the band, again over 3 fabric threads x 3 fabric threads using No 25 Broder. Finish off the thread at the corner and begin again with a waste knot on the next side.

Embroider herringbone stitch on the 4 fabric thread band left between the hemstitching, working from one group of stitches over to the other — use No 20 Broder. See 'Corner Embellishments' for the needleweaving which is worked as a continuation of the herringbone stitching.

Corner embellishments

When you come to a corner, needleweave over all four bars and take the thread back under one bar ready to commence herringbone stitch on the next side.

When you have completed the 2 rows of antique hemstitching and the herringbone stitch, leave 1 fabric thread and work satin stitch pyramids over 2 fabric threads to 6 fabric threads in No 16 Broder up to the needlewoven bar (see diagram).

The last satin stitch pyramid ends at the needlewoven bar. To fill in the large void in the corner

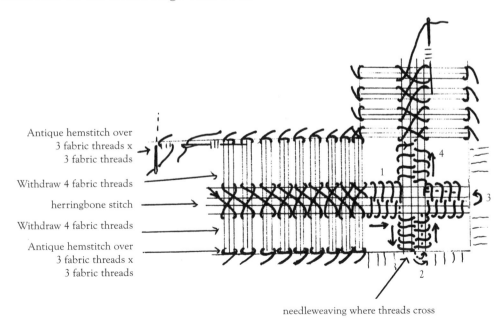

Antique hemstitch over
3 fabric threads x
3 fabric threads

Withdraw 4 fabric threads

herringbone stitch

Withdraw 4 fabric threads

Antique hemstitch over
3 fabric threads x
3 fabric threads

needleweaving where threads cross

work 10 buttonhole stitches to the corner and 10 along the other side grading the first and last 3 stitches (see diagram).

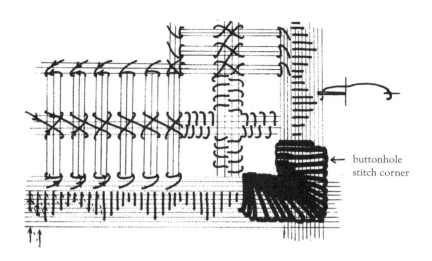

buttonhole stitch corner

OUTER HEM

Ensure all 4 sides are cut on the grain of the fabric. Withdraw 1 fabric thread and cut along this guide-line to neaten any crooked seams and cut off the selvage edges.

To correctly hem the cloth you will need 3 tack-ing lines 45 fabric threads from the edge, another 47 fabric threads, and the third 50 fabric threads.

Withdraw 1 fabric thread on tacking line 2 and one on tacking line 3 to where the tacking lines intersect and weave the thread back into the hem approximately 1cm (^{2}/$_5$"), taking the thread to the

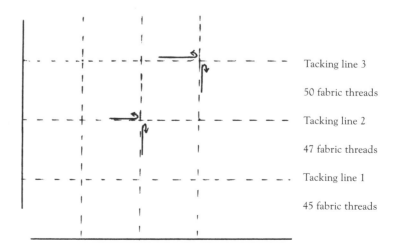

Tacking line 3

50 fabric threads

Tacking line 2

47 fabric threads

Tacking line 1

45 fabric threads

back of the cloth and trimming off any excess thread. Retain the withdrawn thread and use it to sew up the mitred corner. Although it is a heavy thread it will be less noticeable than a sewing cotton.

Double backstitch edge

This stitch gives a very neat and strong edge to a hem. See Stitch Glossary.

In the withdrawn thread space on tacking line 2, embroider double backstitch over 3 fabric threads, using No 16 Broder. Gently pull the thread after the second backstitch. You may have to adjust the number of threads at the corners.

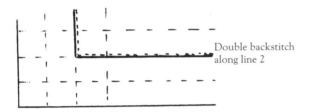

Double backstitch along line 2

MITRED CORNERS

Before cutting the fabric, draw this diagram on a sheet of paper. Fold in the hem and mark the section to be cut to make sure you cut along the correct line.

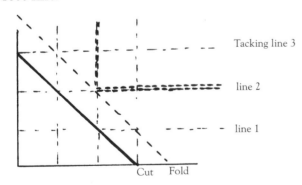

Tacking line 3

line 2

line 1

Cut   Fold

Fold in the hem to the withdrawn thread on line 3 and press the seam. Sew up the mitred corners with the excess fabric thread from the hem, using ladder stitch.

Finish off the hem with antique hemstitch over 3 fabric threads using No 25 Broder.

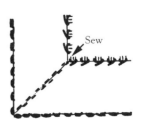

Sew

SCHWALM SAMPLER

*The completed Schwalm embroidery sampler
measures 16cm (6½") by 52cm (21").*

TECHNIQUES

Surface stitches, pulled fabric, drawn thread,
needlelace and needleweaving.

REQUIREMENTS

Belfast 30 count 'oatmeal' linen DMC Catalogue
   No 3609 14053 30cm (12") x 70cm (28")
1 Ball No 12 Ecru Perle Cotton
1 Ball No 8 Ecru Perle Cotton
1 Skein each of No 12, 16 and 20 Ecru Coton-à-
   Broder
Sharp fine pointed small scissors
No 22 Tapestry Needle
No 7 Crewel Needle
Tacking thread medium tone
30cm (12") of calico 90cm (36") wide
Tracing paper or similar and pencil

PREPARING THE FABRIC FOR THE SAMPLER
To prepare the fabric and transfer the design, overlock or zigzag around the edge of the fabric. Mark
with vertical centre of the fabric with a tacking line.
Count 96 threads on both sides of this centre tacking line and also mark with a tacking thread.
Measure 8cm (3⅕") from the top of the fabric and

mark with a horizontal tacking line. The top motif will be placed immediately below this line.

Cut 4 calico strips 10cm (4") wide and sew to all sides of the fabric. Mount firmly in a square or oblong frame with adjustable roller ends.

STITCHES

Surface stitches include chain, coral, buttonhole, herringbone, satin and fly stitch. Leaves, tendrils and stems are completed in coral stitch. All pulled fabric and drawn thread work motifs are surrounded with at least chain and coral stitch, and, as in the 'heart', can include a wide border using herringbone stitch, then another row of coral stitch outside the herringbone stitch, and finish off with open buttonhole stitch semi-circles, accentuating the points and curves. See 'Stitch Glossary' for details.

Special note: How to achieve a neat woven edge on drawn thread border.

For this type of woven edge you need (a) an even number of threads to be withdrawn and (b) the border to be slightly less than half the width of the drawn thread panel.

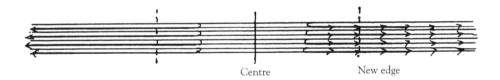

Centre   New edge

To begin, cut at the centre of the threads to be withdrawn.

Cut only threads to be withdrawn

Working one side and one thread at a time, leave thread No 1 and withdraw thread No 2 completely by removing sufficient thread to grip firmly, then withdraw the thread pulling carefully towards the centre of the fabric.

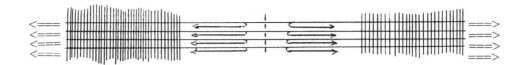

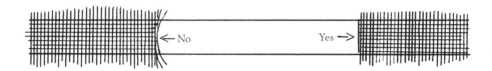

Thread No 1 thread in a blunt needle and weave the thread up and down in the space left by the withdrawing of thread No 2, being careful not to pull it too tight, otherwise the edge will curve.

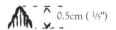

When No 2 has been woven back to the edge, leave No 3 and completely withdraw No 4, weave No 3 back into the space left by the removal of No 4.

Continue until all threads have been removed and replaced, then work the other side in the same manner.

Note: Don't be tempted to withdraw more than one thread at a time. The spacing of the replacement threads will determine the neatness of the finish. This type of darning is only suitable on fabrics that have not been dyed after weaving. Dyed fabrics will have spots of the base colour left on the threads.

SECTION 1 — PINE CONES AND FLOWER
Use No 7 Crewel needle for chain and coral stitch, for most other stitches use No 22 Tapestry needle.

Using No 16 Broder chain stitch on the outline of the pinecones and the main flower.

Using No 16 Broder and coral stitch embroider the stems, tendrils, outside chain stitch on the 2 pinecones and the main flower. Work open buttonhole semicircles at base of flower, 2 sets of 4 adjoining buttonhole circles and semicircles at the top of the flower using No 16 Broder.

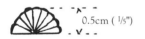

0.5cm (1/5")

0.5cm (1/5")

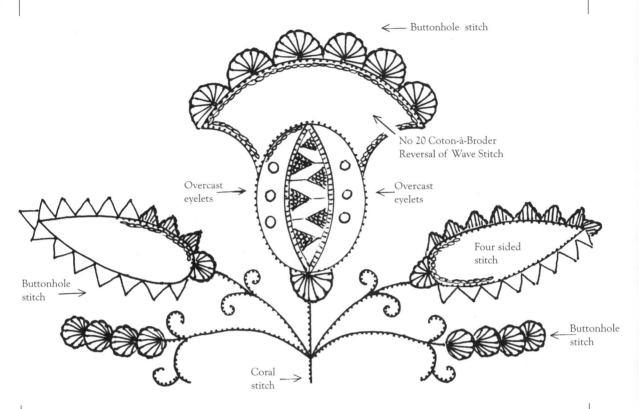

Buttonhole stitch

No 20 Coton-à-Broder
Reversal of Wave Stitch

Overcast
eyelets

Overcast
eyelets

Four sided
stitch

Buttonhole
stitch

Buttonhole
stitch

Coral
stitch

Pinecones

Using No 16 Broder embroider buttonhole pyramids around the chain and coral stitch outline.

Fillings — using No 20 Broder work four sided stitch.

Compensate for half and quarter stitches along the edges.

Main Flower

Fan at the top of the flower — withdraw 1 thread, leave 3 threads weft only.

To withdraw threads, cut one thread at a time in the centre of the motif, take the thread to the wrong side of the fabric, remove to the edge and cut as close as possible to the fabric.

Embroider using No 16 Broder and the reversal of wave stitch working over 4 fabric threads.

Oval section of flower — either side of the needlelace centre embroider 3 overcast eyelets using No 20 Broder.

Needlelace centre — outline in buttonhole stitch with the pearl edge towards the centre where the fabric will be cut away, using No 12 Perle cotton. Also using No 12 Perle cotton embroider the buttonhole pyramids each side taking the thread to the opposite side to complete the pyramid and take the thread through the back of 3 buttonhole stitches to begin the next pyramid.

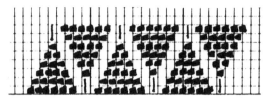

Lace fillings — Buttonhole stitch Pyramids

SECTION 2 — BANDS

Band 1

Leave 8 fabric threads. Beginning from the left work fly stitch with the stem of the fly stitch over 3 fabric threads and the 'v' section horizontally over 3 fabric threads and vertically over 4 fabric threads using No 8 Perle cotton and No 22 tapestry needle. Using the same thread and needle embroider straight stitches over 4 fabric threads every 4 fabric threads. Leave 3 fabric threads and withdraw the next 4 fabric threads, leave 3 fabric threads and withdraw the next 4 fabric threads.

Work antique hemstitch using No 20 Broder over first 3 horizontal fabric threads and 48 groups of 4 threads. Embroider Italian hemstitching using No 20 Broder over the centre 3 fabric threads line.

Using No 20 Broder work antique hemstitch over 3 horizontal fabric threads and 48 groups of 4 threads.

Using No 16 Broder work raised chain band over 4 x 4 fabric threads.

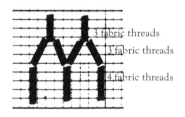

3 fabric threads
3 fabric threads
4 fabric threads

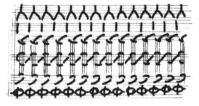

Fly Stitch
Straight Stitch
Antique Hemstitching
Italian Hemstitching
Antique Hemstitching
Raised Chain Band

Band 2

Leave 5 threads.

Using No 8 Perle Cotton embroider 2 straight stitches over 3 fabric threads and 2 straight stitches over 6 fabric threads beginning in the centre with 2 straight stitches over the 6 fabric threads.

Leave 3 fabric threads and withdraw the next 16 fabric threads.

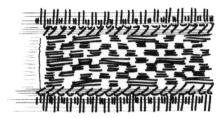

Straight Stitch
Antique Hemstitching

Needleweaving

Antique Hemstitching
Straight Stitch

Using No 20 Broder embroider antique hemstitch over 3 fabric threads — 64 groups top and bottom of the 16 fabric threads.

Using No 8 Perle Cotton embroider 2 straight stitches over 3 fabric threads and 2 straight stitches over 6 fabric threads beginning in the centre with 2 straight stitches over the 6 fabric threads.

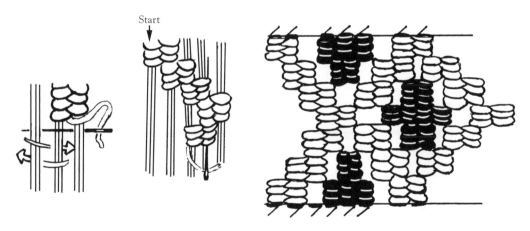

Start

Needleweave over the withdrawn section of threads beginning in the centre.

The dark section of the needleweaving is embroidered using No 16 Broder and the light zigzag section in No 8 Perle Cotton.

Begin with Perle Cotton in the centre, fastening the thread in the back of the hemstitch.

Band 3

Leave 11 fabric threads and withdraw the next 2 fabric threads, then leave 3 fabric threads, withdraw the next 8 fabric threads, leave 3 fabric threads and withdraw the next 2 fabric threads.

Begin with the 3 fabric threads left in the band, work Italian hemstitching over 4 fabric threads — 48 groups both top and bottom of the band.

Next, using No 8 Perle cotton, embroider a fly stitch variation immediately above and below the Italian Hemstitching, working over 4 vertical threads and 8 horizontal threads — 24 repeats.

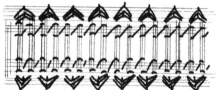

Fly Stitch Variation
Italian Hemstitching

Italian Hemstitching
Fly Stitch Variation

SECTION 3 — CIRCLES AND BANDS

Three Circles

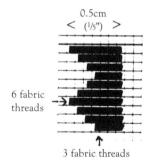

Leave 17 fabric threads and transfer the circles to the fabric placing one on the centre line of the sampler and 2 evenly spaced between the tacking line and the centre. Using No 16 Broder, chain stitch around each circle, then coral stitch outside the chain.

Circle A (left)

Outside the chain and coral stitch, using No 8 Perle cotton, embroider straight stitch pyramids evenly around the circle, making sure the stitches do not lean over but point towards the centre of the circle.

Filling — Withdraw 2 fabric threads, leave 2 fabric threads both warp and weft and, using No 8 Perle cotton, embroider rose stitch in the centre.

0.5cm
< (1/5") >

6 fabric
threads

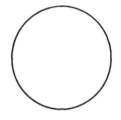

3 fabric threads

Circle B (centre)

Outside the chain and coral stitch, using No 8 Perle cotton, embroider individual chain stitches over 6 fabric threads.

Filling — Withdraw 2 fabric threads and leave 2 fabric threads both warp and weft. Using No 20 Broder embroider first lattice stitch on the grid, then 3 needlewoven bars on each block, working diagonally across the circle.

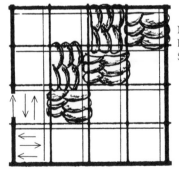

Circle C (right)

Outside the chain and coral stitch, using No 8 Perle cotton, embroider straight stitches (i.e. 2 short over 3 fabric threads and 2 long over 6 fabric threads) evenly around the circle.

Filling — Withdraw 2 fabric threads, leave 2 fabric threads both warp and weft. Using No 8 Perle cotton, needleweave basket filling stitch working 3 needlewoven bars over each grid.

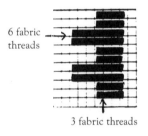

6 fabric threads →

3 fabric threads

Needleweave Basket Filling Stitch

Band 4

Leave 18 fabric threads and withdraw 18 fabric threads.

On both sides of the withdrawn panel, using No 20 Broder, embroider antique hemstitch over 3 fabric threads, grouping 3 threads = 64 groups.

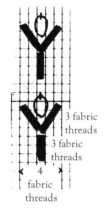

3 fabric threads

3 fabric threads

4 fabric threads

Embroider 'rosebuds' either side of the hemstitch. Leave 2 fabric threads and embroider fly stitch using No 8 Perle cotton, working from left to right on the top row and from right to left on the bottom row. Then add one chain stitch in the 'V' of the fly stitch.

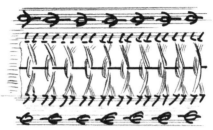

Fly Stitch and Chain Rosebuds

Antique Hemstitching

Twisted Bars and Wrapped Centre Thread

Antique Hemstitching

Fly Stitch and Chain Rosebuds

Three Squares

Leave 7 fabric threads and, from the centre thread of the sampler, count 14 threads either side. The three squares are 29 x 29 threads. The tendrils, buttonhole eyelets and single chain leaves are embroidered using No 16 Broder.

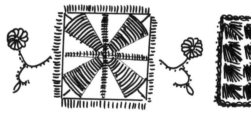

Square A (left)

Outline the square, using No 16 Broder, first with chain then with coral stitch.

Filling — Leave 6 fabric threads and withdraw 1 fabric thread both warp and weft (leaving 1 fabric thread next to the chain). Using No 20 Broder and beginning at the top left corner work satin stitch diagonally across the defined square.

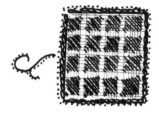

Diagonal Satin stitch

Square B (centre)

Outline the square in buttonhole stitch (with the pearl edge towards the centre) using No 16 Broder. Carefully cut the fabric inside the square. Using No 16 Broder lay 2 threads in the centre from the top to the bottom and needleweave over these 2 threads. Slip the needle through the back of the buttonhole to the other side and again lay 2 threads and needleweave across these threads.

Buttonhole Stitch over 3 fabric threads

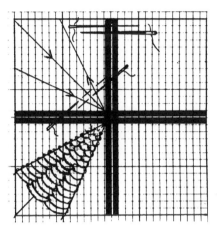

Next, halfway between the centre and the edge (¼ of the square) lay 1 thread from the top edge to the centre and back to ¼ distance on the left side. Take the thread to the back of the buttonhole to the centre and lay another thread to the centre of the square. Needleweave across these 3 threads to the outer edge. Work the remaining 3 corners in the same manner.

Square C (right)

Outline the square using No 16 Broder first in chain stitch then coral stitch. Leave 6 fabric threads and withdraw 1 fabric thread both warp and weft (leaving 1 fabric thread next to the chain). Using No 20 Broder and satin stitch, work a diagonal fan beginning at the top left corner.

Satin stitch Fan

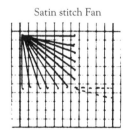

SECTION 4 — BANDS

Band 5

Leave 16 fabric threads, withdraw 6 fabric threads, leave 10 fabric threads and withdraw the next 6 fabric threads.

Use No 8 Perle cotton for all stitches on this band.

To group the threads work buttonhole pyramid fans. The first fan begins 4 threads from the side, then every 8 threads thereafter, finishing 4 threads from the end.

Work the 9 buttonhole stitch pyramid fans over 10 vertical fabric threads and 8 horizontal fabric threads. Needleweave 7 times over 4 fabric threads and under 4 fabric threads taking the needle back up through the needleweaving and the fan to begin the next needlewoven bar. *Note:* The needleweaving must begin and end with needleweaving over 2 fabric threads and under 2 fabric threads as in diagram.

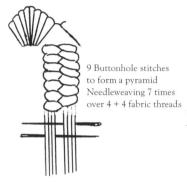

9 Buttonhole stitches
to form a pyramid
Needleweaving 7 times
over 4 + 4 fabric threads

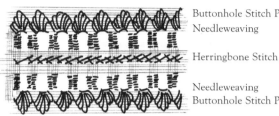

Buttonhole Stitch Pyramid Fans
Needleweaving

Herringbone Stitch

Needleweaving
Buttonhole Stitch Pyramid Fans

Work herringbone stitch in the centre of the 10 fabric thread band, over 4 fabric threads x 4 fabric threads. Complete the other side of the band the same as above.

Band 6

Leave 8 fabric threads. Use No 8 Perle cotton for this band. Embroider straight stitch pyramids over 9 fabric threads beginning in the centre with the longest stitch over 9 fabric threads, the next over 8 fabric threads, next over 7 fabric threads and so on until you have 7 stitches. Then increase by 1 fabric thread each stitch until you cover 9 fabric threads. Leave 7 fabric threads and repeat the above border. In the centre of the 7 threads, work 2 running stitches over 5 fabric threads and under 7 fabric threads, then weave a thread through the 2 running stitches without piercing the fabric.

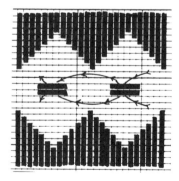

Straight stitch pyramid

Woven running stitch

Straight stitch pyramid

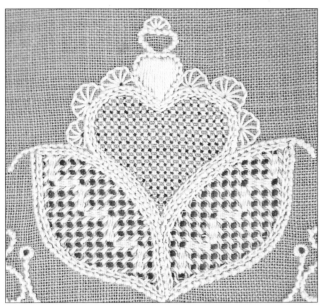

8. Detail —
Heirloom Cloth Flower 3

9. Detail —
Heirloom Cloth Flower 4

10. Detail —
Heirloom Cloth Flower 5

11. Detail —
Heirloom Cloth Flower 6

12. Detail —
Heirloom Cloth Flower 7

13. Detail —
Heirloom Cloth Flower 8

14 SAMPLER

15. Detail — Sampler Section 1

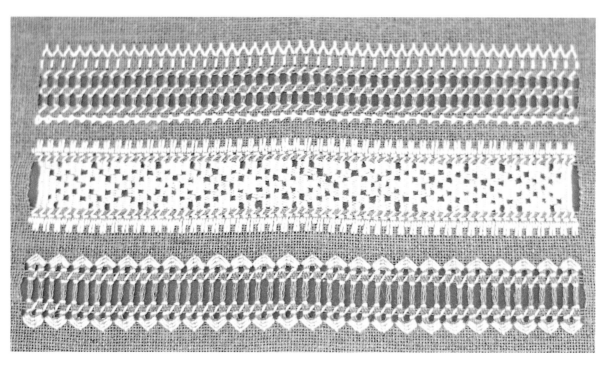

16. Detail — Sampler Section 2

Band 7

Leave 13 fabric threads, withdraw 6 fabric threads, leave 4 fabric threads and withdraw 6 fabric threads.

Using No 20 Broder work antique hemstitch over 3 fabric threads grouping 4 fabric threads = 48 groups. Work the antique hemstitch on the other side next, but begin and end with a 2 fabric thread group to stagger the groups. Over the 4 fabric threads in the centre, work herringbone stitch using No 16 Broder, splitting the hemstitch group by taking 2 threads from one group and 2 threads from the next group.

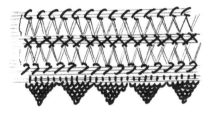

Antique Hemstitch

Herringbone Stitch

Antique Hemstitch
Needlelace — Buttonhole
Stitch Pyramids

Needlelace edge

Using No 12 Perle cotton, work buttonhole stitch over 3 horizontal fabric threads, miss 2 vertical fabric threads (repeat) = 96 buttonhole stitches. To work the pyramid, into the first 6 buttonhole stitches of the above row work a further 6 buttonhole stitches to the right. Working buttonhole stitch backwards, work 5 to the left, 4 to the right, 3 to the left, 2 to the right and one final buttonhole to complete the pyramid. To take the thread back to begin the next pyramid, overcast down the right hand side back to the base buttonhole. Work 16 buttonhole pyramids across the sampler.

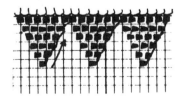

See page 50 for further details on needlelace edge.

Buttonhole stitch

← Coral stitch

Wave stitch

Wave stitch

Rose stitch

Buttonhole stitch →

SECTION 5 — HEART, BUDS AND PIGEONS

Heart

The centre of the heart should be placed 5cm (2") or 60 fabric threads below the needlelace pyramids. Transfer the design to the fabric.

On the inner heart outline, using No 16 Broder, work a row of chain and using No 12 Broder work one row of coral outside the chain, beginning at the point marked on the small heart diagram. Work a row of herringbone stitch using No 16 Broder, then another row of coral stitch and buttonhole stitch semicircles, emphasising the base of the heart and the top of the heart as indicated. See diagram page 43.

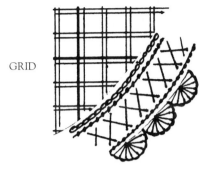

GRID

Detail of heart filling
surrounded by the
following rows:
Chain
Coral
Herringbone
Coral
Buttonhole semicircles

Filling — To prepare the grid, leave 2 fabric threads, cut the next 2 either side, as shown in diagram.

Cut these 2 fabric threads, leave 2 fabric threads either side of these 2, cut the next 2 = Cut 2 fabric threads, leave 2 fabric threads both warp and weft, as shown in diagram.

Using No 20 Broder work rose stitch diagonally, working from the top left across to the bottom right hand side.

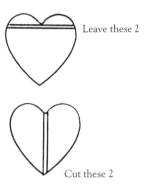

Leave these 2

Cut these 2

Stems, Tendrils and Eyelets

Using No 16 Broder embroider the stems and tendrils in coral stitch, then the eyelets in buttonhole stitch.

Buds

Using No 16 Broder, outline the buds first with chain stitch and then coral stitch with a buttonhole semicircle between the coral stitch stem and the bud.

Filling — Leave 3 fabric threads and withdraw 1 fabric thread weft only. Using No 20 Broder embroider wave stitch compensating for half stitches at the edge.

Pigeons

Transfer the pigeon design to the fabric and outline using No 16 Broder and chain stitch. On the inside of the wing, embroider 3 buttonhole semicircles.
Beak — 2 straight stitches.
Eye — 1 small cross stitch.
Feet — 1 long straight stitch and 3 small straight stitches at the end to form the claw.

PINCUSHION, SCISSOR TAG AND NEEDLECASE

The pincushion measures 17cm (6 ⁴/₅") square, including a 2.5cm (1") wide needlelace edge. Scissors tag measures 5cm (2") diameter and the needlecase measures 6cm x 9cm (2 ²/₅" x 3 ³/₅").

TECHNIQUES

Surface stitches, pulled fabric, drawn thread work and needlelace.

REQUIREMENTS

Belfast 30 count 'oatmeal' linen DMC Catalogue
    No 3609 14053 20cm x 50cm (8" x 20")

1 ball No 8 ecru Perle Cotton

1 skein each of No 12, 16 & 20 ecru
    Coton-à-Broder

No 22 Tapestry & No 7 Crewel Needle

Lining fabric 20cm x 50cm (8" x 20")

Baby flannel or similar for needlecase leaves
    13.5cm x 18cm (5²/₅" x 7¹/₅")

Flannelette 14cm x 14cm (5³/₅" x 5³/₅")

Iron on interfacing 9cm x 13.5cm (3³/₅" x 5²/₅")

Calico 20cm x 44cm (8" x 17³/₅")

Card 1mm thick, 6cm x 28cm (2²/₅" x 11¹/₅")

1 jug or pony bead for closure or small button with
    shank

Small quantity of fibre filling for pincushion

Medium tone tacking thread

Ecru sewing thread and general sewing needle

Sharp fine pointed small scissors

Round embroidery frames 18.5cm (7") and
    10cm (4") diameter

Tracing paper or similar and pencil

Dry glue stick (instant adhesive)

Dressmaking pins

Fine sandpaper to smooth edges of card

Cord weight (2 heavy washers and paper clip)

Pinking sheers to edge needlecase leaves

Stanley knife or similar and metal rule

PREPARING THE FABRIC

See the following page for placement of pattern
pieces on your fabric. Cut the pieces of linen, lining, interfacing, flannelette, flannel and calico with
scissors. Cut the card using a Stanley knife or craft
knife and a metal rule, cutting on a thick pad of
newspapers to prevent damage to surfaces. Place the
pieces in separate plastic bags carefully labelled
'pincushion', scissors tag' and 'needlecase'. This
may save you a lot of work reconstructing a jigsaw
of bits and pieces at a later date.

Overlock, zigzag or oversew around the edge of
your linen pieces to prevent fraying.

STITCHES

Stitches include chain, coral, buttonhole, overcast,
lattice, Russian drawn thread filling and satin stitch.
Stems and tendrils are completed in coral stitch.
All drawn thread work motifs are surrounded with
chain and coral stitch. See Stitch Glossary for
details.

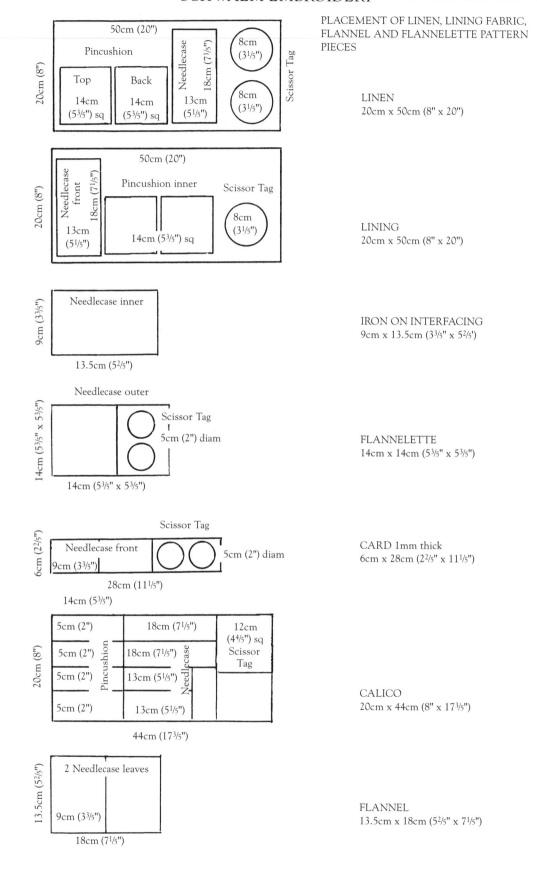

PLACEMENT OF LINEN, LINING FABRIC, FLANNEL AND FLANNELETTE PATTERN PIECES

LINEN
20cm x 50cm (8" x 20")

LINING
20cm x 50cm (8" x 20")

IRON ON INTERFACING
9cm x 13.5cm (3³/₅" x 5²/₅')

FLANNELETTE
14cm x 14cm (5³/₅" x 5³/₅")

CARD 1mm thick
6cm x 28cm (2²/₅" x 11¹/₅")

CALICO
20cm x 44cm (8" x 17³/₅")

FLANNEL
13.5cm x 18cm (5²/₅" x 7¹/₅")

Russian Drawn Filling stitch

Overcast Eyelet

Lattice stitch

Chain stitch   Coral stitch

Padded Satin stitch

72 Buttonhole stitches

Four-sided stitch over 2 fabric threads x 2 fabric threads = Total 70 Four-sided stitch

PINCUSHION

At this stage you will only need one piece of the pincushion linen which should be overlocked or zigzagged around the edge. Mark with a tacking thread the centre of the fabric both vertically and horizontally. To form the square count 72 threads either side of these centre vertical and horizontal lines and mark with a tacking thread.

Using the method outlined on page 8, transfer the above design to your fabric making sure the perimeter lines match up with your tacking threads.

Once your design is transferred you need to attach the 4 calico strips to the linen (5cm, 2" wide x 14cm, 5⅗" long) using a straight machine stitch.

Then mount the linen in a square or 18.5cm (7")
diameter frame.

Using No 20 Broder and No 24 tapestry needle
begin with a four-sided stitch over 2 fabric threads
x 2 fabric threads, starting and ending 2 fabric
threads inside the tacking thread i.e. 70 x four-sided
stitches on each side.

EMBROIDERY ON THE PINCUSHION

Use No 7 crewel needle for coral stitch, and No 22
tapestry for all other embroidery stitches.

To embroider the pincushion, begin with chain
stitch and No 20 Broder to outline the 4 hearts and
the centre circle, working just inside the tacking
thread. You can now remove the tacking thread
from the centre circle and the 4 hearts only.
Embroider coral stitch using No 16 Broder outside
the chain stitch of the hearts and circle.

Using No 16 Broder and coral stitch embroider
the stems and tendrils including the small stem to
the bud. (Leave the 8 buds until later as you will
use a finer thread around the edge of the satin
stitch).

Buds

Using No 12 Broder and satin stitch, first pad the
oval shape with satin stitches going the length of
the oval, then across the oval. Outline with coral
stitch using No 20 Broder.

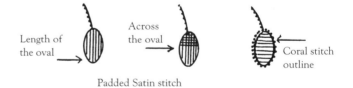

Length of
the oval →   Across
the oval →   Coral stitch
outline

Padded Satin stitch

Eyelets

Refer to page 15 of Heirloom Cloth.

Circle

You have already embroidered the chain stitch with
No 20 Broder and coral stitch with No 16 Broder
around the circle.

Now work the Pyramids around the circle using No 16 Broder. These are comprised of 5 button-hole stitches over 4 fabric threads for the shortest stitch, over 5 fabric threads for the middle stitch and over 6 fabric threads for the longest stitch.

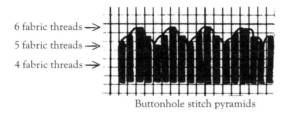

6 fabric threads →
5 fabric threads →
4 fabric threads →

Buttonhole stitch pyramids

To withdraw threads

Cut one thread at a time in the centre of the motif, take the thread to the wrong side of the fabric, remove to the edge and cut as close as possible to the fabric. Follow the instructions in the next paragraph for the number of warp and weft threads to be removed and the spacing between these threads.

Circle Centre — Beginning with the 2 centre fabric threads warp and weft withdraw these 2 fabric threads and leave 2 fabric threads either side, working across the circle until a grid is formed.

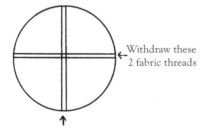

Withdraw these
2 fabric threads

Using No 16 Broder work Russian Drawn Filling stitch (see Stitch Glossary) beginning on the left hand side of the circle and work diagonally across the circle, then turn the embroidery around and work the next row again diagonally across the circle from left to right.

Hearts — Using the method already described in withdrawing threads to form the above grid, leave the 2 fabric threads marked on the diagram and withdraw 2 fabric threads either side. Using No 16 Broder work lattice stitch over the withdrawn grid (see Stitch Glossary for instructions).

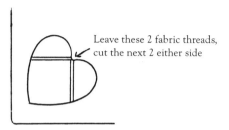

Leave these 2 fabric threads, cut the next 2 either side

Needlelace Edge

Prepare the fabric ready for the needlelace by embroidering buttonhole stitch over 2 warp fabric threads and 2 weft fabric threads using No 8 Perle cotton. You should have a total of 72 buttonhole stitches each side. The last buttonhole stitch on each side is worked diagonally across the corner.

If you look at the photograph of the completed pincushion you will see the details of the needlelace edge. Outside the four-sided stitch border, there are 72 buttonhole stitches on each side, then 16 buttonhole stitch pyramid groups around the edge.

Needlelace Pyramids

New thread

The 6 pyramid groups are worked with one long thread approximately 1m (40") in length, using No 8 Perle cotton and a tapestry needle. If you have to bring in a new thread make sure it is introduced in one of the buttonhole stitch loops.

Pyramids Stage 1

Row 1 — work 6 buttonhole stitches going into the loop of the previous buttonhole row from left to right.

Row 2 — working from right to left embroider 5 buttonhole stitches into the previous buttonhole loops beginning the 2nd stitch in from the needle.

Row 3 — working from left to right work 4 buttonhole stitches into the previous buttonhole stitch loops beginning the 2nd stitch in from the needle.

Row 4 — working from right to left work 3 buttonhole stitches into the previous buttonhole stitch loops beginning the 2nd stitch in from the needle.

Row 5 — working from left to right work 2 buttonhole stitches into the previous buttonhole stitch loops beginning the 2nd stitch in from the needle.

Row 6 — working from right to left work the final 1 buttonhole stitch and hold the pyramid in place with a pin.

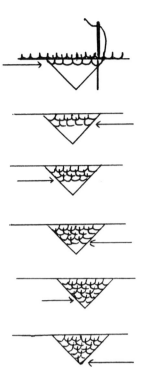

STOP — READ THE FOLLOWING TIP

Place a pin into the last buttonhole stitch to hold the pyramid in place while you take the thread back to the base buttonhole row and leave this pin in place until you have worked the buttonhole stitch on the semi-circle to the pin only. (You do not work the semi-circle yet. This information has only been provided at this stage so that you know when the pin can be removed).

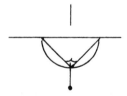

To get back to the base buttonhole stitch row so that you can work the next pyramid, weave the thread down the right side of the pyramid.

Work 2 more pyramids taking the thread back to A after completing the 3rd pyramid.

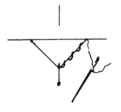

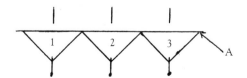

Pyramids Stage 2

Working from right to left, take the thread from A under the pin in 3, back into the base buttonhole stitch row between pyramid 2 and 3, under the pin in 2, and back into the base buttonhole stitch row between pyramid 1 and 2. Then under the pin in 1 and finally back into the 1st buttonhole stitch in the base row.

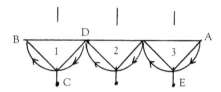

Buttonhole stitch from left to right over this thread until you reach pin 1. Remove the pin. Buttonhole stitch over the thread and into the loop of the last buttonhole stitch in pyramid 1 at C, then over the thread back to D. Buttonhole stitch over the thread until you reach E. *Note:* Do not work from E to A — this will be the very last section to complete the entire group).

Pyramids Stage 3

You now have to lay a base thread for the next row of 2 pyramids — take the thread from E into the last buttonhole at the centre of pyramid 2 and across to the last buttonhole at the centre of pyramid 1.

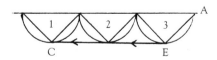

Pyramids Stage 4

Working from left to right work pyramid 4, then pyramid 5 the same as in the 1st row, weaving the thread down the side of pyramid 5 back to E to begin the loops. Take the thread from E to the left between pyramid 4 and 5 and on to C as previously described.

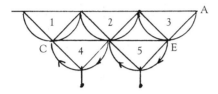

Pyramids Stage 5

Buttonhole stitch back to F *only* — removing pins as previously described.

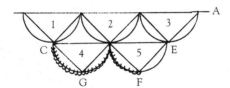

Pyramids Stage 6

Lay a base thread for the last pyramid from F to G, and work pyramid 6.

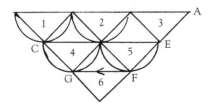

Pyramids Stage 7

Take the loop thread from F to G under the pin and buttonhole stitch back to F, then to E and back to A.

Work 3 more pyramid groups along this side of the pincushion.

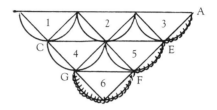

Pyramids Stage 8

When you reach the corner and have worked the first row of buttonhole pyramids, embroider a bar to link one side of the pincushion to the next at stage 2.

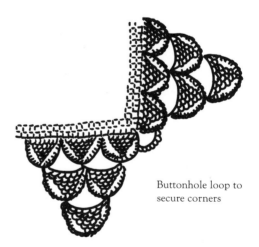

Buttonhole loop to secure corners

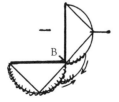

Buttonhole stitch from B halfway between B and the pin. Run a thread into a buttonhole stitch halfway along the loop of pyramid 3 in the previous group and buttonhole stitch back across this loop to the buttonhole stitch loop and continue working this pyramid and group.

When you have completed all 16 groups, press the embroidery by placing it face down on a thick towel and using a damp pressing cloth, gently press down on the embroidery. Leave aside to dry completely.

Cut the fabric 5 fabric threads outside the base buttonhole stitch row being careful not to cut the needlelace edge. Turn the fabric under and hold in place using ecru sewing thread and backstitch into the four-sided stitch holes working from the right side of the linen.

Pincushion Back

Mount the linen in a frame and mark the perimeter only the same as the top. Work the four-sided stitch over 2 fabric threads x 2 fabric threads using No 20 Broder, the same as the top. Cut the linen 10 fabric threads outside the four-sided stitch. Work buttonhole stitch over 2 fabric threads x 2 fabric threads through both thicknesses using No 8 Perle cotton. Trim excess fabric to remove bulk in the corners and press. Using ecru sewing thread stitch the top and bottom together along 3 sides only, stitching into the pearl edge of the buttonhole stitch from the back and the fabric from the top.

Turn the
fabric under
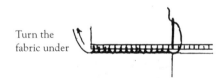

Pincushion Inner Padding

Straight machine stitch around the edge of the 2 x 14cm (5³⁄5") squares of lining fabric, using a 1.5cm (³⁄5") seam allowance and leaving an opening for the filling. Turn out and press. Fill with fibre filling until it measures 2.5cm (1") in thickness through the centre. Do not over fill.

Close the opening. Place filled pad in the pincushion and close the opening.

SCISSOR TAG

The 8cm (3^1/$_5$") square of linen will need to be over-locked or zigzagged around the edge and stitched into a larger square of calico. Cut away a 7cm (2^4/$_5$") square of calico from behind the linen. This will allow you to secure the fabric in a 10cm (4") diameter frame.

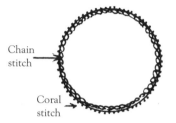

Chain stitch

Coral stitch

The embroidery in the centre of the scissor tag is identical to the pincushion centre. Trace the circle from the pattern to the linen. Embroider chain stitch using No 20 Broder just inside the tacking thread, remove tacking thread and then work coral stitch using No 16 Broder outside the chain stitch.

Pyramids around the circle

Using No 16 Broder work pyramids made up of 5 buttonhole stitches over 4 fabric threads for the shortest stitch, over 5 fabric threads for the middle stitch and over 6 fabric threads for the longest stitch (see diagram).

Buttonhole stitch pyramids

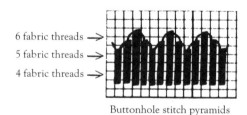

6 fabric threads →
5 fabric threads →
4 fabric threads →

Buttonhole stitch pyramids

Drawn thread filling

Beginning with the centre fabric threads, both warp and weft, withdraw 2 fabric threads and leave 2 fabric threads across the circle.

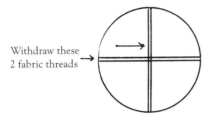

Withdraw these
2 fabric threads →

Using No 16 Broder, work Russian Drawn Filling stitch beginning on the left hand side and working diagonally across the circle, then turn the embroidery around and work the next row again working diagonally across from left to right.

To assemble the Scissor Tag

Cut another piece of linen 8cm (3¹/₅") square and 1 lining fabric 8cm (3¹/₅") square

Cut 2 pieces of card 5cm (2") in diameter and use fine sandpaper to smooth the edge of the card. Using dry glue, stick flannelette to one side only of the 2 cards and trim off excess flannelette to the edge of the card.

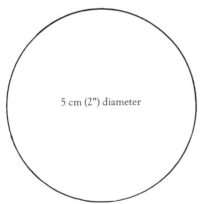

5 cm (2") diameter

Next cover one card only with lining fabric. Cut an 8cm (3¹/₅") diameter circle out of the lining fabric and with tacking thread and running stitch 1 cm (²/₅") in from the edge run a gathering thread around the circle. Place the card flannelette side down on the lining fabric and draw up the gathering thread then lace across the circle to tighten.

Cut the embroidered linen into a circle, 8cm (3¹⁄₅") in diameter and using running stitch gather the linen over the card. (The lining fabric should show through the drawn thread circle). Cover the other circle with linen in the same manner.

Match up the grain of the fabric on both circles and stitch together taking approx 3 fabric threads from one circle, then going across to the other circle and take 3 fabric threads. (Tip: hold both pieces together while working around the edge).

Leave a 1cm (²⁄₅") opening to hide the ends of the cord.

To make a cord

Measure around the circle then add 15cm (6") to go from the tag to the scissors and back to the tag = 30cm (12") total. Multiply the 30cm (12") x 2.5 = 75cm (30"). The thread should be 75cm (30") long. Using a pencil to twist the thread (No 8 Perle cotton) stand 75cm (30") from another person holding a pencil or a cuphook, and take the thread around the pencils 3 times (total of 6 threads between the 2 pencils). Secure the beginning and end of the thread with a knot. If using 1 pencil and a cuphook, while maintaining tension on the thread, turn the pencil in your hand until the thread begins to buckle. To check if the thread has been twisted enough, release the tension and the thread will twist into a firm cord — resume tension on the thread. While maintaining tension of the thread, place the weight in the centre of the cord and hold away from the pencil and cuphook. Take the pencil end to the cuphook end and release the tension on the weight. The thread will naturally ply to form a cord. Knot the pencil and cuphook ends of the thread together and trim away the 1st knot and excess thread.

The method is very similar if 2 people are turning pencils. Both turn clockwise and the thread will twist.

Place the knot from the end of the cord in the 1cm (²⁄₅") opening of the tag and pin the cord in place. Using a matching sewing thread (ecru) sew the cord (sew through the cord not over it) onto the edge of the tag beginning at the opening. Take the cord around the edge of the tag, back to the

1cm (⅖") opening and leave a loop that will be secured around the scissors. Place the end of the cord in the opening and secure. Attach to the scissors by looping the cord through the handle.

NEEDLECASE

The embroidery on the needlecase is an adaptation of a corner of the pincushion. Attach strips of calico to all sides of a 13cm x 18cm (5⅕" x 7⅕") piece of linen. Trace and tack the design to the fabric 2.5cm (1") in from the bottom right hand corner and mount this corner in the 18.5cm (7") diameter frame.

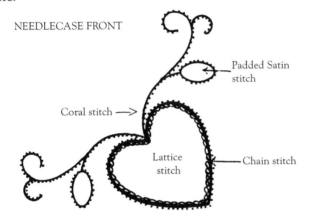

NEEDLECASE FRONT

Padded Satin stitch

Coral stitch →

Lattice stitch

Chain stitch

Using No 20 Broder work chain stitch just inside the tacking thread for the heart and remove the heart tacking thread only. Using No 16 Broder work coral stitch outside the chain stitch and on the stems including the small stem to the bud. The buds are worked in padded satin stitch using No 12 Broder and outline with coral stitch in No 20 Broder as described in the pincushion instructions. Using No 16 Broder work lattice stitch over the withdrawn grid.

Needlecase Outer

Cut 2 pieces of card 9cm x 6cm (3⅗" x 2⅖") and one piece of flannelette 9cm x 14cm (3⅗" x 5⅗"). Dry glue card to flannelette leaving a 2cm (⅘") space between the 2 cards. Trim the flannelette to the edge of the card.

Place flannelette and attached card, flannelette side down on the 13cm x 18cm (5⅕" x 7⅕") lining

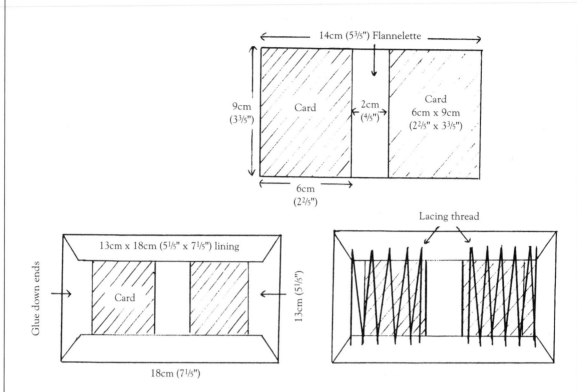

18cm (7¹/₅")

fabric. Dry glue the 2 ends and when dry lace the sides down. The stitches should be about 1cm (²/₅") apart. Start a new thread for each side so as not to distort the spine of the needlecase.

Next, cut back the calico edge on the linen to approx 1cm (²/₅") width. Place the above lining fabric down on the linen placing the embroidery 1cm (²/₅") from the edge of the card, and glue down the 2 ends. Lace the sides of the needlecase working into the calico and a new thread for each side.

Needlecase Inner

Cut interfacing 9cm x 13.5cm (3³/₅" x 5²/₅") and iron on to lining fabric 13cm x 18cm (5¹/₅" x 7¹/₅"). Fold and iron under the edges of the lining fabric to 9cm x 13.5cm (3³/₅" x 5²/₅").

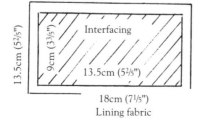

18cm (7¹/₅")
Lining fabric

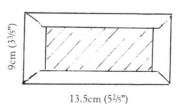

Fold and iron under the edges of the lining fabric

13.5cm (5²/₅")

Cut baby flannel into 2 pieces 9cm x 13.5cm (3³/₅" x 5²/₅") and then trim with pinking shears back to 8cm x 13cm (3¹/₅" x 5¹/₅"). Align to the centre of the lining fabric and using backstitch and ecru sewing thread, attach the flannel down the centre.

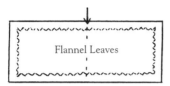

As you will note the lining measures 9cm x 13.5cm (3³/₅" x 5²/₅") and the outer 9cm x 14cm (3³/₅" x 5³/₅"). The 0.5cm (¹/₅") difference is eased into the spine and allows the needlecase to close easily.

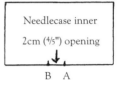

Beginning at A stitch the soft lining to the outer using a matching sewing thread and ladder stitch, sew to B, leaving a 2cm (⁴/₅") opening at the bottom of the spine.

Cord trim

Following the instructions outlined in the Scissor Tag on how to make a cord (page 58), measure the perimeter of the scissor case (46cm, 18²/₅") + 2cm (⁴/₅") for closure and 2cm (⁴/₅") allowance to conceal the end = 50cm (20").

Multiply the 50cm (20") x 2.5 = 125cm (50") is the length of the thread (No 8 Perle cotton) from the pencil to the cuphook = 125cm (50") x 6 lengths of thread. Twist and ply in the manner already described.

To attach the cord, hide the knotted end in the spine between A and B and sew through the cord not over it, working from the lining side to the outer side. It may help to pin the cord in place.

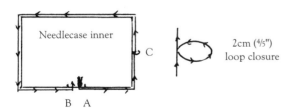

Stop at C which is the centre of the card and make a 2cm (⁴/₅") loop in the cord for the closure. Continue attaching the cord until you reach B.

If you have an excessive amount of cord, knot the cord and hide approx 2cm (⁴/₅") plus the knot, in the spine of the needlecase. Close the spine securely.

Closure

Using No 8 Perle cotton wrap the jug (pony) bead, taking the thread up through the centre, leaving tag to hold onto, and secure the thread in the centre of the bead when it is completely covered.

Jug (pony)
bead

Use the end tag to attach the bead to the front of the needlecase on the edge between the embroidery and the edge of the cord.

Close the needlecase and check the length of the flannel leaves. They may have to be trimmed so that they do not extend beyond the lining fabric.

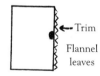

Trim

Flannel
leaves

REPEATING DESIGNS SUITABLE FOR BEGINNERS

*The linen hand towel measures 37cm x 59cm
(14⁴/₅" x 23³/₅") and the soap/hosiery bag
measures 19cm x 16cm (7³/₅" x 6²/₅").
The commercial towelling hand towel measures
40cm x 60cm (16" x 24") and has an
embroidered band measuring 40cm x 9cm
(16" x 3³/₅").*

Techniques

Surface stitches and pulled fabric.

Requirements

Belfast 30 count 'oatmeal' linen DMC Catalogue
No 3609 14053:
   40cm (16") x 70cm (28") for linen hand towel
   42cm (16⁴/₅") x 11cm (4²/₅") for band for commercial towel
   40cm (16") x 17cm (6⁴/₅") for soap/hosiery bag
Lining fabric for soap/hosiery bag, 36cm x 17cm
   (14²/₅" x 6⁴/₅")
2 skeins of No 12 ecru Coton-à-Broder
2 skeins of No 16 ecru Coton-à-Broder
1 skein of No 20 ecru Coton-à-Broder
No 22 tapestry needle
No 7 crewel needle

Medium tone tacking thread

Ecru sewing thread and general sewing needle

Tracing paper or similar and pencil

Adjustable square frame of 18.5cm (7") diameter frame

Ecru No 8 Perle cotton, stranded cotton for cord, or ribbon plus weight to make the cord.

PREPARING THE FABRIC

Cut the pieces of linen as illustrated. Overlock, zigzag or oversew the edge of the linen pieces to prevent fraying.

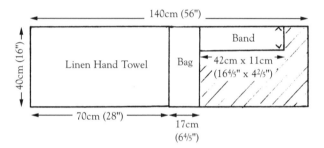

Mark with a tacking thread the centre of the linen for the hand towel. The bird design is placed 14cm ($5^{3}/_{5}$") from the bottom of the hand towel. The circles and hearts are placed in the centre of the 42cm x 11cm ($16^{4}/_{5}$" x $4^{2}/_{5}$") band and the heart is placed 10cm (4") from the top of the 40cm x 17cm (16" x $6^{4}/_{5}$") strip.

STITCHES

Surface stitches include chain, straight (single satin stitch) coral, herringbone, buttonhole, feather, chevron and backstitch. Pulled fabric stitches include chequer filling, four-sided, overcast, and pin stitch.

17. Detail — Sampler Section 3

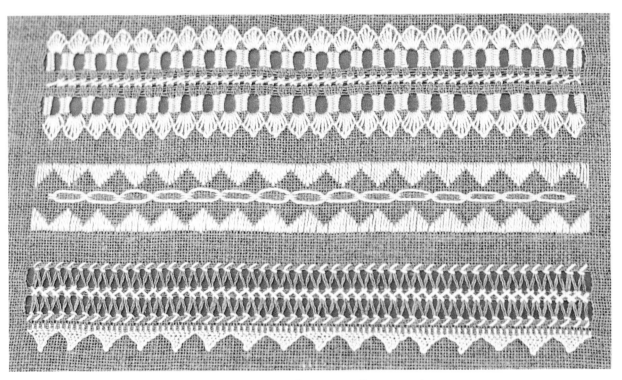

18. Detail — Sampler Section 4

19. Detail — Sampler Section 5

20 Pincushion, scissors tag and needlecase

21 Repeating designs suitable for beginners

22 TEA COSY, TABLE CENTRE OR CLOTH DESIGN WITH NEEDLELACE EDGE AND
SERVIETTE WITH NEEDLELACE FEATURE

Linen hand towel

This design could be repeated around the hem of a skirt, edge of a cloth or cushion (using a heart in the corners) mirror image the birds and repeat the design down the front of a waistcoat, a shirt or on curtains or tiebacks for curtains.

Linen measures 40cm (16") wide x 70cm (28") long. The birds are placed towards the bottom of the linen. Mark the vertical centre of the fabric and

repeat here

Design with detail

Design outline

14cm (5³/₅") up from the bottom with a tacking thread.

Using the method outlined on page 8 transfer the design to your fabric, making sure the line below the birds is straight.

Mount the fabric in a large square/oblong frame or an 18.5cm (7") diameter frame.

With No 16 Broder outline the birds including the wing with chain stitch. Using No 12 Broder embroider coral stitch outside the chain stitch on the wings and outline the 4 tail feathers also with coral stitch.

Five buttonhole semicircles are embroidered along the curved section of the wing with No 16 Broder. Three buttonhole pyramids for the crest, 2 straight stitches for the eye and 2 straight stitches for the beak in No 20 Broder.

Embroider 2 backstitches for the legs and 3 straight stitches for the claws also in No 20 Broder.

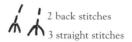

The overcast eyelet feature on the tail feathers is embroidered using No 20 Broder.

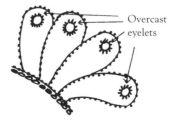

Wing filling

The wing has been given movement by using simple straight stitches in a pulled fabric pattern and No 20 Broder.

Begin where indicated working 10 straight stitches over 3 warp fabric threads, then work 8 straight stitches over 3 weft fabric threads.

Work the next rows either side of this foundation row leaving a square of 3 fabric threads x 3 fabric threads where the stitches change direction.

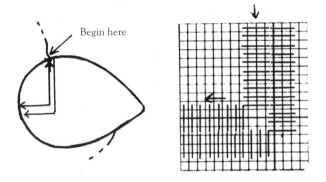

Heart

The centre heart is all worked with No 16 Broder.

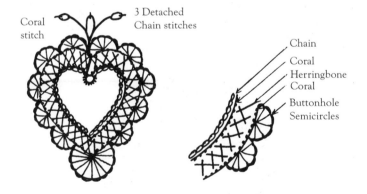

Under the birds claws, using No 20 Broder, work 16 backstitches over 3 fabric threads, beginning 6 backstitches in front of the front claw of each bird (one continuous line will show up any irregularities when you transferred the design to the fabric).

repeat here

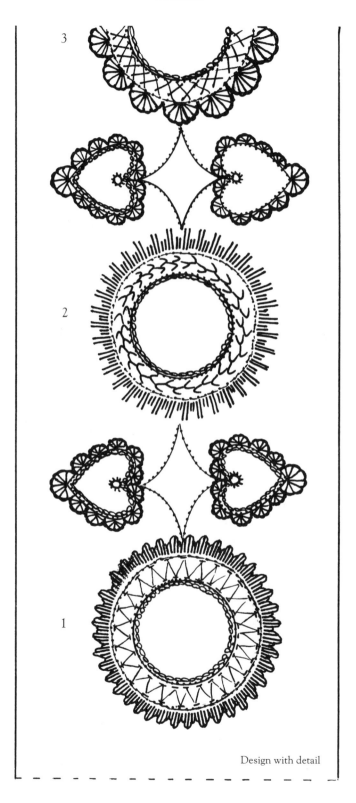

3

2

1

Design with detail

Design outline

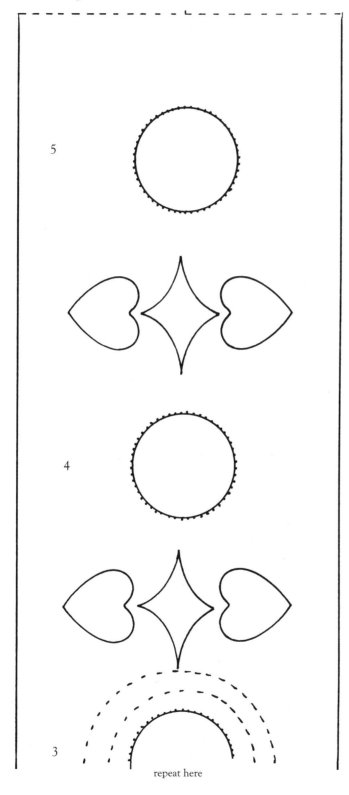

repeat here

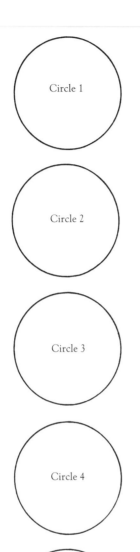

To finish off the towel, remove 1 weft fabric thread 3cm (1⅕") down from the top and another one 12cm (4⅘") up from the bottom. Complete the side seams first by folding under a 1cm (⅖") hem and handstitch by carefully picking up one thread from the background fabric, leave 3 fabric threads and pick up one thread from the hem, continue until all the hem is secured or stitch by machine. Next, fold the fabric to form a 1cm (⅖") hem at the top and a 4cm (1⅗") hem at the bottom. Work pin stitch on both hems from the top, using a sewing thread or a single strand of stranded cotton to match the fabric (see Stitch Glossary).

TOWEL BAND

The circles and hearts design can be used as a border in the centre of a cloth (by placing a heart in each corner), on a long bell pull, on clothing, or as a band for a towel holder.

The linen measures 42cm x 11cm (16⅘" x 4⅖") to fit a 40cm x 60cm (16" x 24") commercial towelling hand towel. Mark the centre of the fabric both vertically and horizontally with a tacking thread.

Following the instructions on page 8, transfer the design.

Mount the fabric in an adjustable square frame or 18.5cm (7") diameter frame.

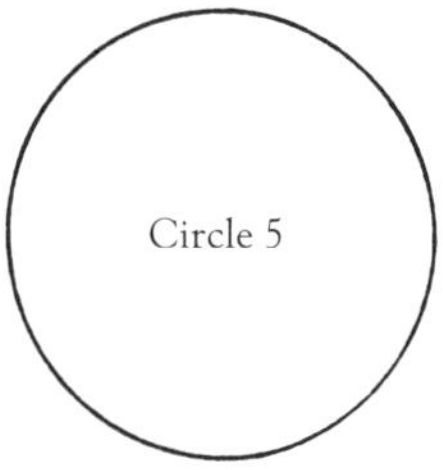

Circles

Using No 16 Broder, outline the circles with chain stitch and using No 12 Broder embroider coral stitch outside the chain stitch.

Circles 1 and 5
Using No 16 Broder embroider chevron stitch outside the chain and coral stitch, then using No 12 Broder coral stitch, followed by an edge of buttonhole pyramids using No 16 Broder.

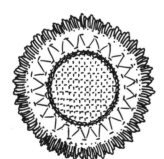

Circles 2 and 4
Using No 16 Broder embroider feather stitch outside the chain and coral stitch, then using No 12
Broder coral stitch, followed by an edge of 2 long
and 2 short straight stitches.

Circle 3
Using No 16 Broder embroider herringbone stitch
outside the chain and coral stitch, then using No 12
Broder coral stitch, followed by an edge of buttonhole stitch semicircles.

Centre of the Circles
Embroider the centre of all 5 circles with four-
sided stitch working over 3 fabric threads both
warp and weft and No 20 Broder. As this is a
pulled fabric filling make sure the thread is pulled
firmly, compensating for half stitches on the edge
of the circle.

Hearts

Using No 16 Broder outline the hearts with chain
stitch and with No 12 Broder embroider coral
stitch outside the chain stitch. Outside the coral
stitch embroider small buttonhole semicircles,
accentuating the point at the base of the heart. At
the top of each of the hearts embroider an overcast
eyelet using No16 Broder.
  The link between the circles and the hearts is
embroidered with coral stitch using No 12 Broder.

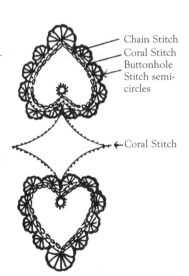

Chain Stitch
Coral Stitch
Buttonhole
Stitch semi-
circles

← Coral Stitch

Finishing off

Press the embroidery face down on a very fluffy towel so that you do not flatten your work. Turn under a 1cm (^{2}/5") hem on all 4 sides of the linen and stitch to the towel. Alternatively attach lining fabric approx 3mm inside the hem. Attach press studs, Velcro, ribbon or cord to each end if you are making the towel holder. (Will go around 2 hand towels).

SOAP OR HOSIERY BAG

Fold the fabric in half i.e. 40cm x 17cm (16" x 6^4/5") to 20cm x 17cm (8" x 6^4/5") and tack a line down the centre. The heart is placed 10cm (4") from the top. Lining fabric 36cm x 17cm (14^2/5" x 6^4/5").

Using the method outlined on page 8, transfer the design to your fabric making sure the centre of the design is aligned with the centre of the fabric.

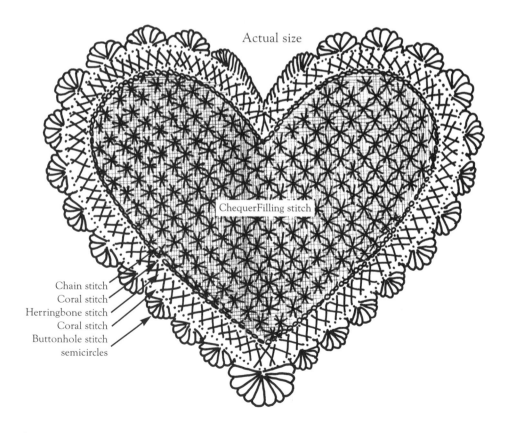

Actual size

ChequerFilling stitch

Chain stitch
Coral stitch
Herringbone stitch
Coral stitch
Buttonhole stitch
semicircles

Using No 16 Broder embroider chain stitch on the heart outline. Outside the chain stitch embroider coral stitch using No 12 Broder, then herringbone stitch using No 16 Broder. Outside the herringbone stitch, work one row of coral stitch in No 12 Broder, followed by buttonhole stitch semicircles in No 16 Broder, accentuating the point at the bottom and the curves at the top of the heart.

Filling

The centre of the heart is embroidered using chequer filling stitch and No 12 Broder. Begin where indicated (see Stitch Glossary for details).

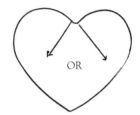

TO ASSEMBLE THE BAG
Cut the lining fabric into 2 pieces 18cm x 17cm (7^{1}/$_{5}$" x 6^{4}/$_{5}$"). Sew with a 1cm (^{2}/$_{5}$") seam the 17cm (6^{4}/$_{5}$") side of the lining pieces with right sides facing each other. Press the seams.

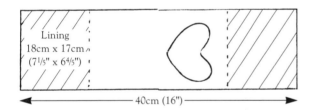

Fold the linen in half with right sides facing. Sew a 1cm (^{2}/$_{5}$") seam from the fold up to the end of the lining and across the top, leaving a 6cm (2^{2}/$_{5}$") opening. Sew up the other side.

Carefully pull the linen through the opening and press seams. (The lining should be 1cm, ^{2}/$_{5}$" below the top of the linen). Close the 6cm (2^{2}/$_{5}$") opening by hand.

Sew 2 seams 2cm (^{4}/$_{5}$") and 3cm (1^{1}/$_{5}$") down from the top for a casing for the cord or ribbon.

Carefully remove seam stitching on the linen only between the 2 casing seams and secure with buttonhole stitch.

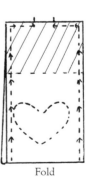

Fold

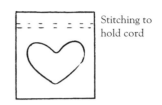

Stitching to
hold cord

Make two 60cm (24") cords and thread them
through the casing in opposite directions and place
a small wooden bead or jug (pony) bead 3cm (1$^1/_5$")
from the end of the cord to hold the cord in place
and fringe the end of the threads.

HOW TO MAKE A CORD
You will need a 60cm (24") cord. To calculate the
length of the thread, multiply the 60cm (24") x 2.5
= 150cm (60").

The thread should be 150cm (60") long. Using a
pencil to twist the thread (No 8 Perle cotton) stand
150cm from another person holding a pencil or a
cuphook, and take the thread around the pencils 3
times (total of 6 threads between the 2 pencils).

See page 58 of Scissors Tag for further details
on how to make a cord.

TEA COSY, TABLE CENTRE OR CLOTH DESIGN WITH NEEDLELACE EDGE AND SERVIETTE WITH NEEDLELACE FEATURE

The tea cosy measures 40cm (16") wide x 28cm (11⅕") high including 2cm (⅘") wide needlelace edge
The serviette measures 36cm (14⅖") square.

TECHNIQUES

Surface stitches, pulled fabric and needlelace. One thread withdrawn for the hemstitch hem on the serviette.

REQUIREMENTS

Belfast 30 count 'oatmeal' linen DMC Catalogue No 3609 14053:

   40cm x 60cm (16" x 24") for tea cosy or table centre

   40cm x 40cm (16" x 24") for each serviette

Lining fabric (inner for tea cosy) 40cm x 120cm (16" x 48")

Wadding 40cm x 60cm (16" x 24")

1 skein of No 12 and 3 skeins of No 16 ecru Coton-à-Broder

Medium tone tacking thread
Sewing thread or stranded cotton to match fabric
Tracing paper or similar and pencil
45cm (18") square frame or round frame
45cm (18") square of calico

PLACEMENT OF PATTERN PIECES FOR THE MOST ECONOMIC USE OF YOUR FABRIC

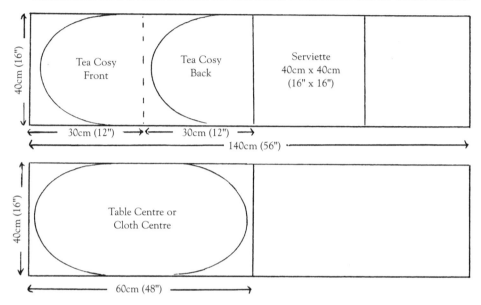

PREPARING YOUR FABRIC
Cut the pieces of linen as illustrated. Overlock, oversew or zigzag around the edge of the linen pieces to prevent fraying.

Mark with a tacking thread the centre of the fabric for the tea cosy front and 3cm (1⅕") from the edge for the base of the pattern, or both vertical and horizontal centre for the table centre. Around the edge of the serviettes, mark with a tacking thread on all 4 sides (see page 91).

See page 77 to adjust the design for a table centre or for a cloth so that the two ends link up.

STITCHES
Surface stitches include chain, coral, straight (single satin stitch) padded satin stitch, herringbone, buttonhole and cross stitch. Pulled fabric stitches include satin stitch blocks, single faggot stitch, overcast eyelets, honeycomb darning stitch and antique hemstitch.

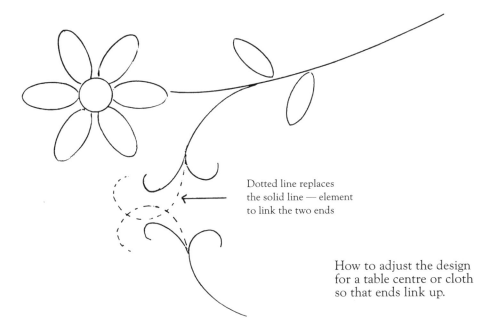

Dotted line replaces
the solid line — element
to link the two ends

How to adjust the design
for a table centre or cloth
so that ends link up.

TEA COSY

This design is made to fit a 4 cup teapot and an adjustment line has been provided for a smaller teapot.

Note: For a tea cosy to keep the teapot warm there must be a pocket of air surrounding the pot, therefore a snug fit will not be as effective as a larger, more generous tea cosy.

The design base outline is placed 3cm (1⅕") from the edge of the fabric. Transfer the design carefully as outlined on page 8.

Begin with the tulip at the top of the design.

Outline sections 1 and 2 first with chain stitch using No 16 Broder and outside the chain stitch with coral stitch using No 12 Broder.

Section 1

Embroider buttonhole semicircles across the top. Mark the outline with running stitch to help with placement of the semicircles. Outside the semicircles using No 16 Broder work coral stitch on the straight lines and an overcast eyelet at the end of each of the lines also in No 16 Broder.

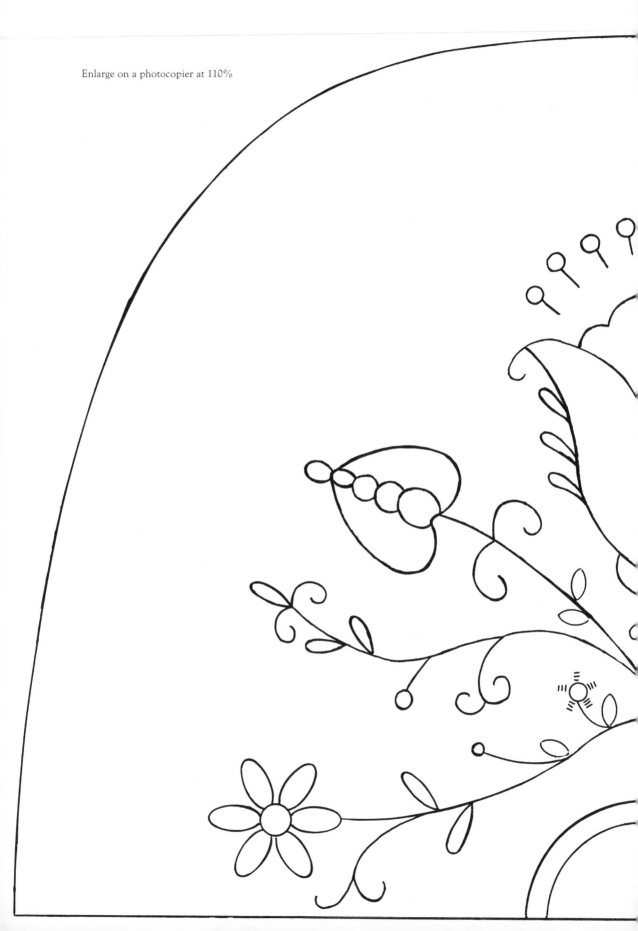
Enlarge on a photocopier at 110%

Enlarge on a photocopier at 110%

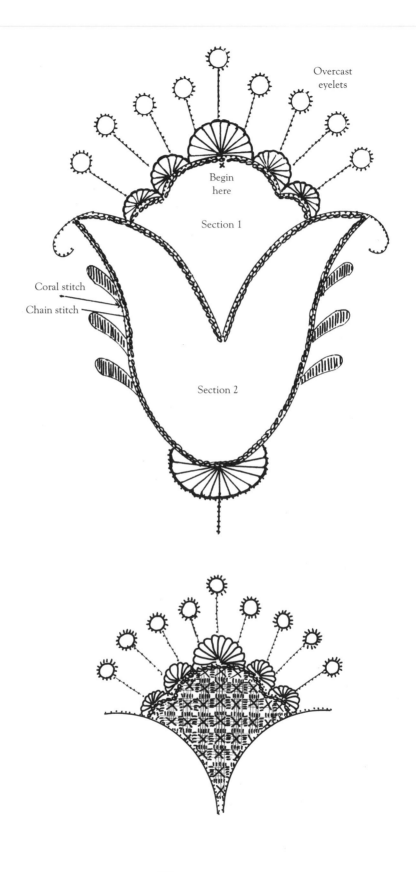

Overcast
eyelets

Begin
here

Section 1

Coral stitch

Chain stitch

Section 2

Filling

Work 5 straight stitches over 3 fabric threads firmly
pulling the threads. Work diagonally beginning at
the centre top. Fill in the squares working diagonally. Be consistent with the crossing of the threads:
/ first then \ or the reverse.

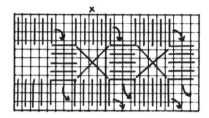

Section 2

Filling

Using No 16 Broder and beginning 3 fabric threads
below the centre dip in the design, work a block of
3 straight stitches over 6 fabric threads, then working either to the left or right, work another 3
straight stitches beginning half way along the last
block.

Leave 3 fabric threads between each row.
Between each block there should be a small 3 fabric
threads x 3 fabric threads square. When you have
completed the satin stitch blocks, work single faggot stitch on the lower edge of the block over the 3
fabric threads. (See also Stitch Glossary)

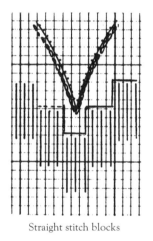

Straight stitch blocks

BDF
G
ACE

Up at A, down at B
up at C, down at D
up at E, down at F
up at G, ...

Embroider a large buttonhole semicircle at the base of the tulip using No 16 Broder and outline this semicircle with coral stitch in No 12 Broder.

Buttonhole stitch
semicircle

The padded satin stitch embellishments either side of the tulip are embroidered using No 12 Broder.

Padded
Satin stitch

Heart Shape Leaves

Outline first with chain stitch in No 16 Broder and outside the chain, work coral stitch in No 12 Broder.

Filling
Work 5 buttonhole circular shapes beginning at the stem and work towards the point.

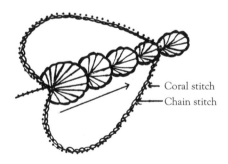

Coral stitch
Chain stitch

Large Flowers

Using No 12 Broder embroider buttonhole stitches along one side around the point and back down the other side of each petal. Work coral stitch also in No 12 Broder around the centre circle.

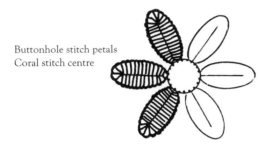

Buttonhole stitch petals
Coral stitch centre

Small flower, stem and leaf

Using No 16 Broder work the coral stitch around the edge of the leaf and fill with satin stitch. Work coral stitch along the stem to the small flower. Then work satin stitch over the circle and five groups of 3 straight stitches around the circle.

Satin stitch centre
Straight stitch petals

Stems, tendrils, leaves and remaining eyelets

Work all remaining stems and tendrils in coral stitch using No 12 Broder. Apart from the leaf with the small flower, all other leaves are outlined with No 12 Broder and filled with satin stitches also in No 12 Broder.

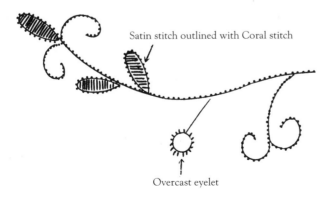

Satin stitch outlined with Coral stitch

Overcast eyelet

Circle or Semicircle

Outline the semicircle with chain stitch using No 16 Broder and embroider coral stitch outside the chain with No 12 Broder

Next, embroider a row of herringbone stitch in No 16 Broder (compensating for the curve by working the outside stitches slightly further apart than those towards the centre of the circle). Using No 12 Broder work coral stitch outside the herringbone and finish off with 2 long straight stitches and 2 short stitches using No 16 Broder.

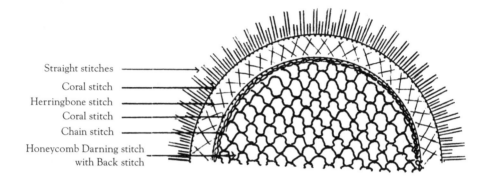

Straight stitches
Coral stitch
Herringbone stitch
Coral stitch
Chain stitch
Honeycomb Darning stitch with Back stitch

Filling

Honeycomb darning stitch with backstitch — see page 106.

This filling is worked over 2 horizontal rows. Pick up 3 fabric threads from the top row and take the needle 3 fabric threads down and pick up 3 fabric threads from the next row. Go back up to the top row and pick up another 3 fabric threads.

Continue in this manner until you reach the end of the row.

The next row adds one further needle movement. Pick up 3 fabric threads from the bottom row and take the needle 3 fabric threads up and pick up 3 fabric threads from the above row. Instead of going down to the bottom row, work one backstitch and bring the needle back out in the same hole. Now take the needle down to the bottom row and pick up 3 fabric threads.

Continue until you complete this row.

To make up Tea Cosy front and back

Turn up a 1cm (²/₅") hem along the base of the tea cosy and carefully hand stitch.

Turn under a 1cm (¹/₅") hem around the edge and using No 16 Broder buttonhole stitch over 3 fabric threads x 3 fabric threads. Do not pull the thread on the curves otherwise the edge will buckle. Press the 2 pieces face down on a thick fluffy non-textured towel. Use a damp cloth if needed but be careful not to burn the linen. Overstitch the front and back together with a sewing thread.

Needlelace edge

If you are unable to hold the fabric in your hand while working the needlelace edge, tack the linen onto a 45cm (18") square of calico and use pins to hold the buttonhole pyramids in place (see page 52 in Pincushion). The pyramid groups are worked first and then the picot edge is added last of all working left to right.

Begin in the centre of the tea cosy and work one pyramid group, then 14 either side working into each of the foundation buttonhole loops.

Total of 29 pyramid groups.

Needlelace Pyramids

The 3 pyramid groups are worked with one long thread approx 1m (40") in length, using No 16 Broder.

Pyramids Stage 1
Refer to page 51 of Pincushion for details on how to work the pyramids stage 1.

Complete the Pyramid
To get back to the base buttonhole stitch row so that you can work the next pyramid, weave the thread down the right side of the pyramid.

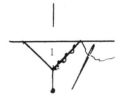

Work 1 more pyramid taking the thread back to A after completing the 2nd pyramid.

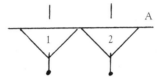

Pyramids Stage 2
Working from right to left, take the thread from A under the pin in 2, back into the base buttonhole stitch row between pyramids 1 and 2. Then take the thread under the pin in 1 and finally back into the 1st buttonhole stitch in the base row.

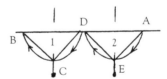

Buttonhole stitch from left to right over this thread until you reach pin 1. Remove the pin. Buttonhole stitch over the thread and into the loop of the last buttonhole stitch in pyramid 1 at C, then over the thread back to D. Buttonhole stitch over the thread until you reach E. (*Do not work from E to A as this will be the very last section to complete the entire group*).

Pyramids Stage 3

You now have to lay a base thread for the next pyramid. Take the thread from E, across to the last buttonhole at the centre of pyramid 1.

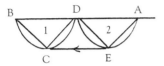

Pyramids Stage 4

Working from left to right work pyramid 3, weaving the thread down the side of pyramid 3, back to E to begin the loop.

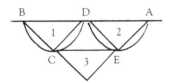

Pyramids Stage 5

Take the thread from E under the pin and into C. buttonhole stitch back to E, and then on to A.

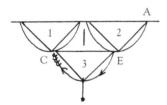

Work 14 more pyramid groups each side of this foundation pyramid.

Picot Edge

With the needlelace edge facing towards you, the picot edge is worked from left to right in a continuous line.

Using No 16 Broder secure the thread under the base buttonhole stitch row and bring the thread out next to the 1st buttonhole stitch loop of pyramid 1.

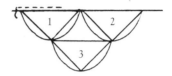

*Leave 3 buttonhole stitches on the loop and take the needle down through the loop of the buttonhole stitch and pull the thread through.

With the needle towards you, place the needle in the loop you have just made, and loop the thread around the needle. Gently pull the thread — a knot will form.

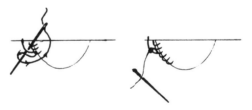

With the needle pointing away from you, place the needle between the 2 threads below the knot and again gently pull the thread to complete the knot.*

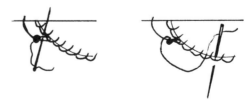

Leave 3 buttonhole stitches and repeat the above steps from * to *.

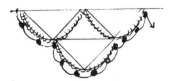

When you need to begin a new thread, finish off the old thread in the buttonhole stitch loop and begin the new thread in one of the other loops as in the diagram.

Bring in
new thread

As you can see from the diagram, these picots should be clearly visible. If they are not, adjust your tension on the thread or use a heavier thread. No 16 Broder is approx the same weight as No 8 Perle so go to No 5 Perle or No 12 Broder. Remember when you use a heavier thread it is more difficult to begin and end threads.

  Press the needlelace edge, face down on a thick fluffy towel.

To make the Tea cosy inner

Cut 4 tea cosy shapes out of the lining fabric and 2 out of the wadding.

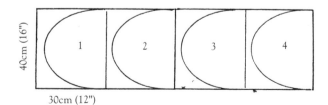
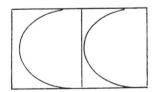

40cm (16")

| 1 | 2 | 3 | 4 |

30cm (12")

Stitch or quilt each wadding piece to a piece of lining fabric.

Place the remaining 2 pieces of lining fabric right sides facing, on top of these. Place one of the quilted pieces wadding side down and the other quilted piece fabric side down.

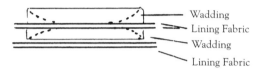

Machine stitch around the top only.

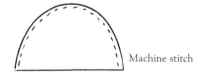

To turn the shape to the correct side, turn the top quilted layer over. The top seam is now encased in the shape.

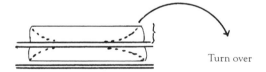

Fit it inside the tea cosy and trim off excess fabric along the base, before closing the bottom seam by hand.

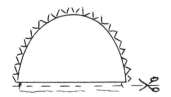

SERVIETTES

Refer to page 76 on preparing your fabric. Around the edge of the serviettes mark with a tacking thread on 4 sides 7 fabric threads in from the edge, 8 fabric threads in from the tacking thread and another 9 fabric threads in from the last tacking thread, i.e. 7 fabric threads in from the edge, 15 fabric threads in from the edge and 24 fabric threads in from the edge.

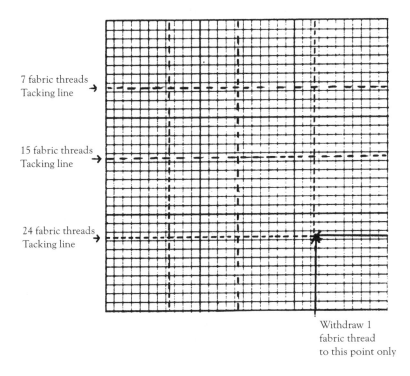

7 fabric threads
Tacking line →

15 fabric threads
Tacking line →

24 fabric threads
Tacking line →

Withdraw 1
fabric thread
to this point only

The corners should look like this.

Next to the tacking thread 24 fabric threads in from the edge cut one thread in the centre and withdraw it only to where the tacking threads cross.

Weave this thread back through the border and trim off any excess.

Weave thread

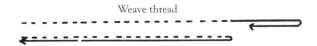

Fold the fabric in on the 7 fabric threads tacking
line so that it is inside the 15 fabric threads tacking
line on all 4 sides.

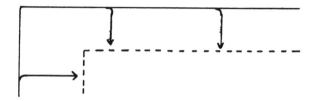

Fold the fabric in again from the 15 fabric threads
tacking line to the inside of the 24 fabric threads
tacking line on all 4 sides.

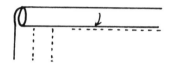

Press the 4 sides carefully. Don't move the iron
back and forward — lift it and place it down on the
next area.

As you will notice you have excessive bulk in
each of the corners. To remove some of the fabric,
open out the fabric and cut the corner off where
the 7 fabric threads and 15 fabric threads tacking
lines intersect. Press down a fold across the corner.

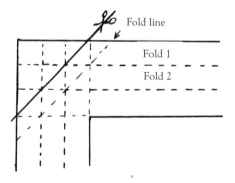

Refold the sides and corners. The corners should
now meet in what is known as a mitred corner.
Using a matching sewing thread carefully close the
corner taking up 2 threads from one side, then 2
threads from the other. Do not oversew — the
stitches should be invisible.

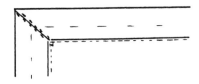

Tack down the hem so that you can see the with-drawn thread ready to begin the hemstitching.

Antique hemstitch hem

With the hem towards you, begin and end the thread under the fold with 2 or 3 running stitches and a backstitch to lock the thread. Begin 5cm (2") out from a corner and work into the space left by the withdrawn thread.

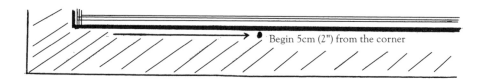

Begin 5cm (2") from the corner

Working from left to right, bring the thread out 1 fabric thread into the hem.

Take the needle from R-L under 3 fabric threads and pull the thread through.

Under 3 fabric threads

To complete the stitch, take the needle under the hem and out 1 fabric thread into the hem 3 fabric threads from the last stitch in the hem.

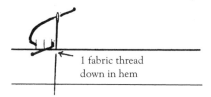

1 fabric thread down in hem

You should now have two small holes where the thread has been withdrawn. Continue in this manner until you are approximately 2cm (⁴/₅") from the corner. Check that you have multiples of 3 fabric threads. If you do not, adjust the next stitch to 4 fabric threads or down to 2 fabric threads to ensure the last stitch has 3 fabric threads. Continue the hemstitch around the corner, checking each corner until you are back to where you began. Again check the number of fabric threads and adjust before you reach the end.

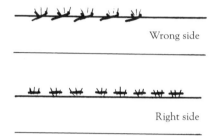

Wrong side

Right side

Needlelace Trim

The needlelace across the corner of the serviette is something different. However, you may choose to embroider one of the motifs.

Measure two sides, 10cm (4") out from the corner and mark with a pin. Measure across the corner between the hemstitched hem. This should measure 13.5cm (5²/₅"). Tack a line along this 13.5cm (5²/₅") line carefully noting the cross grain of the fabric.

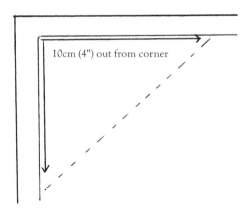

10cm (4") out from corner

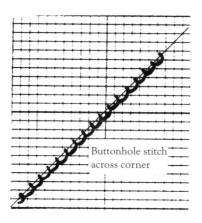

Buttonhole stitch across corner

Using No 16 Broder, work 1 row of buttonhole stitch from left to right. The buttonhole stitch is worked into every fabric threads across and 3 fabric threads down. Count the number of buttonhole stitches and divide by 6. This will give you the number of base pyramids. It should be an even number. If it is not an even number, adjust the space between the pyramids i.e. leave 2 base buttonhole stitches between the pyramids to allow room for the semicircles. Remember allow room for your needlelace — don't squash in just one more. 6 pyramid groups should fit comfortably across the 13.5cm (5²/₅").

Follow the instructions for the buttonhole pyramids and the picot edge on page 88.

Press face down on a thick fluffy non-textured towel.

ADDITIONAL DESIGNS

Suitable for embroiderers who have some experience in Schwalm embroidery. You are not obliged to adhere to the suggested interpretations of the designs. Transfer the basic outline and embroider them to your own personal taste.

SMALL DESIGN SUITABLE FOR

A PINCUSHION OR BOX TOP

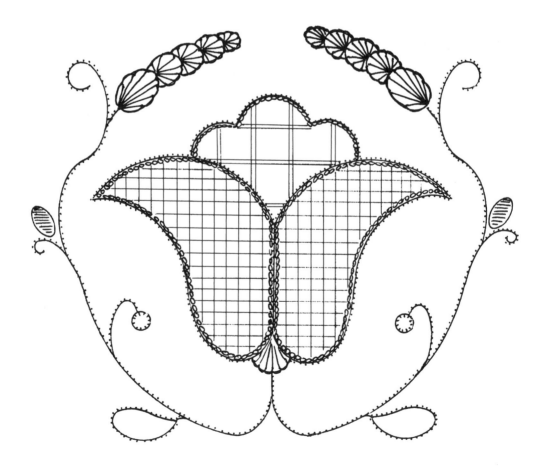

SMALL DESIGN SUITABLE FOR
A PINCUSHION OR BOX TOP

DESIGN SUITABLE FOR A TABLE CENTRE

OR ENLARGE THE DESIGN FOR THE

CENTRE OF A CLOTH

The centre circle can be outlined with chain stitch, coral stitch and buttonhole stitch semicircles.

    The centre of the circle can be left unworked or filled with reticella style needlelace.

DESIGN SUITABLE FOR A 35CM (14") SQUARE CUSH-
ION, 35CM (14") DIAMETER ROUND CUSHION, TABLE
CENTRE OR CENTRE OF A CLOTH

Enlarge on a photo-
copier at 110%

DESIGN SUITABLE FOR A 35CM (14") SQUARE CUSH-
ION, 35CM (14") DIAMETER ROUND CUSHION, TABLE
CENTRE OR CENTRE OF A CLOTH

Enlarge on a photo-
copier at 110%

DESIGN SUITABLE FOR A PICTURE OR IT CAN BE
REPEATED ON BOTH ENDS OF A TABLE RUNNER,
ON FOUR SIDES OF THE CENTRE OF A CLOTH
(WITH THE TULIPS POINTING TOWARDS
THE CENTRE)

DESIGN SUITABLE FOR A PICTURE OR IT CAN BE
REPEATED ON BOTH ENDS OF A TABLE RUNNER,
ON FOUR SIDES OF THE CENTRE OF A CLOTH
(WITH THE HEARTS POINTING TOWARDS THE
OUTSIDE EDGE OF THE CLOTH)

STITCH GLOSSARY

ANTIQUE HEMSTITCH

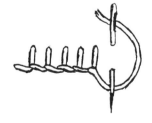

BACKSTITCH

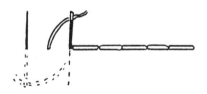

DOUBLE BACKSTITCH

BUTTONHOLE STITCH

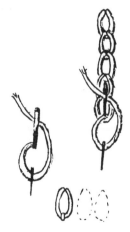

BUTTONHOLE STITCH PYRAMID

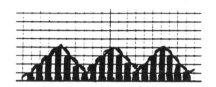

BUTTONHOLE SEMICIRCLES

CHAIN STITCH

CHEQUER FILLING STITCH

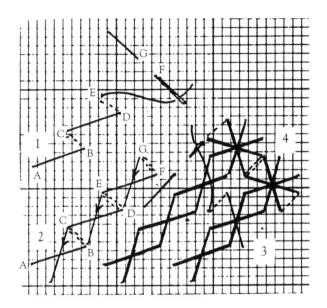

CHEVRON STITCH

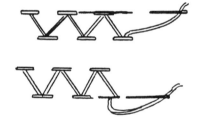

CORAL STITCH

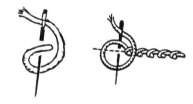

CROSS STITCH

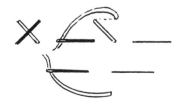

DOVE'S EYE STITCH

FEATHER STITCH

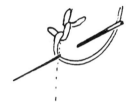

FLY STITCH

FLY STITCH VARIATION

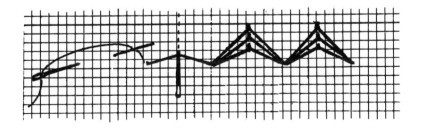

FOUR-SIDED STITCH

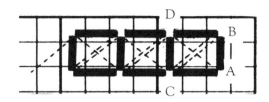

Needle up at A, down at B, up at C, down at A, up at D, down at B, up at C, down at D, up at E...

HERRINGBONE STITCH

HONEYCOMB DARNING STITCH WITH BACKSTITCH

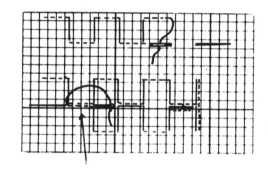

ITALIAN HEMSTITCHING

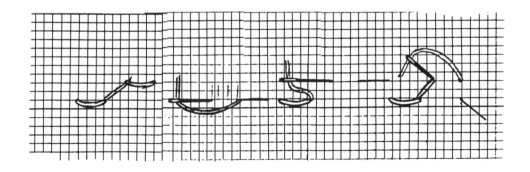

LADDER STITCH

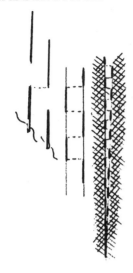

LATTICE STITCH

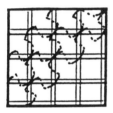

NEEDLEWEAVING ON LATTICE STITCH GRID

OVERCAST EYELET (SEE ALSO PAGE 16)

PIN STITCH

Working over 3 fabric threads, the needle goes up at A, down at B and up at A (pull the thread so that a hole appears at A and B) down at B and up at C.

Next stitch — down at A, up at D, down at A, up at D, down at A, up at E.

Note: The 2 vertical stitches are in the same holes.

RAISED CHAIN BAND

RUNNING STITCH

RUSSIAN DRAWN FILLING STITCH/ROSE STITCH

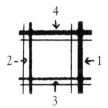

Worked diagonally over 4 arms.

    The thread comes up through the centre of the square, over the right arm 1, back up through the centre and crossing over the thread to the left arm 2.

    Then up through the centre below the above stitches and, to lock the above stitches, place the needle down through the centre from the above stitches, and bring the needle under the lower arm 3. The thread comes over 3 and right over arm 4, with the thread coming out in the top left corner of the threads. The next stitch locks the 4 arms. Insert needle at the bottom right corner and bring it out in the centre of the next diagonal square.

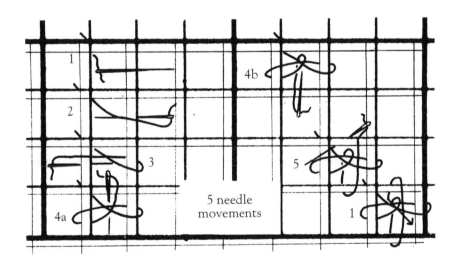

SATIN STITCH (SEE STRAIGHT STITCH)

SATIN STITCH BLOCKS

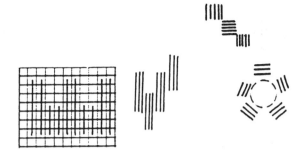

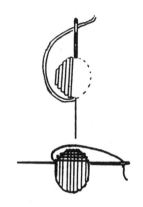

PADDED SATIN STITCH

SECURING THREAD ENDS

SINGLE FAGGOT STITCH

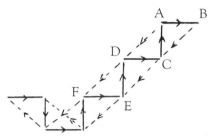

Needle up at A,
down at B
Up at C, down at A
Up at D, down at C
Up at E, down at D
Up at F, down at
E...

STRAIGHT STITCH

STRAIGHT STITCH — SINGLE SATIN STITCH

TWISTED BORDER

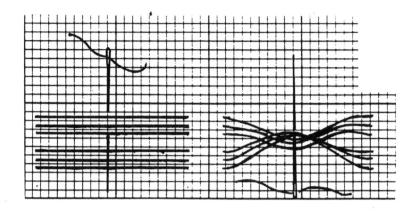

WAVE STITCH

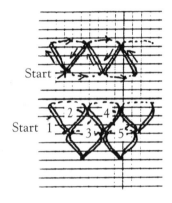

REVERSAL OF WAVE STITCH

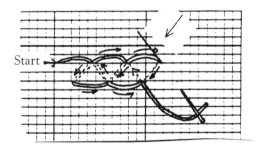

(similar to lattice stitch working on the straight not diagonally)